Learning Right from Wrong in the Digital Age

An Ethics Guide for Parents, Teachers, Librarians, and Others Who Care about Computer-Using Young People

Doug Johnson

Linworth
PUBLISHING, INC

Library of Congress Cataloging-in-Publication Data

Johnson, Doug, 1952-
  Learning right from wrong in the digital age : an ethics guide for
parents, teachers, librarians, and others who care about computer-using
young people / Doug Johnson.
       p. cm.
Includes bibliographical references and index.
  ISBN 1-58683-131-3
  1. Internet and children—Moral and ethical aspects. 2. Computers and
children—Moral and ethical aspects. 3. Cheating (Education) 4.
Internet in education. 5. Internet—Safety measures. I. Title.
  HQ784.I58J65 2003
  004.6'78'083—dc21
                              2003043320

Published by Linworth Publishing, Inc.
480 East Wilson Bridge Road, Suite L
Worthington, Ohio 43085

ISBN: 1-58683-131-3

5 4 3 2

Table of Contents

Table of Contents

Foreword

Much to my children's embarrassment, I've never been shy about letting people know when I find their behavior impolite. My kids burrow a little deeper in their movie theater seats when I tell the talkers in front of us to pipe down. My son tries to look as unrelated to me as possible when I tell a group that its bad language is offensive. I've been known to explain to dog owners why they should pick up after their dogs, to students why they should say please and thank you to cafeteria helpers, and to smokers why they should really believe signs that say "No Smoking." My children don't understand why I am not popped in the nose on a regular basis.

I don't really enjoy these little fits of Miss Mannerism, but I am firmly convinced that if everyone rationally admonished others of their anti-social behavior when they saw it, we would soon be living in a far more civilized world. As educators, the job of teaching polite, and more importantly, ethical behaviors is not an option, but our duty. As parents, we owe it to our children to teach them that ethical behaviors, both practiced and expected, make for happier lives.

 What ethical issues are of the greatest concern to you:

- as a library media specialist?
- as a teacher?
- as a school official?
- as a parent?
- as a community member?

What ethical issues are the most confusing or difficult for you to deal with:

- as a library media specialist?
- as a teacher?
- as a school official?
- as a parent?
- as a community member?

 Percent of ninth graders who used a computer at home in 2001:

M—90%, F—91%

— from *Minnesota Student Survey*, Minnesota Department of Children, Families, and Learning

As we, adults, provide opportunities for children to gain online access to the Internet, we must also take it upon ourselves to learn what our children are doing, to understand what real and imagined dangers our children might encounter, and to articulate a set of values to our children about technology use. In a time when our children always seem to be two steps ahead of us technologically, that is not always easy.

As both an educator and parent, I have learned to stress the consideration of principles rather than relying on a detailed set of rules when working with young learners.

Although sometimes more difficult to enforce in a consistent manner, a set of a few guidelines rather than a lengthy set of specific rules is more beneficial to students in the long run. By applying guidelines rather than following rules, children engage in higher level thinking processes and learn behaviors that will continue into other classrooms, their homes, and their adult lives. Here are mine:

List here any general guidelines you already use with your students or children.

For example: *Your classroom behavior needs to be such that others can do their work without interruption.*

_____

_____

_____

_____

_____

_____

_____

_____

_____

_____

_____

_____

_____

_____

_____

_____

Johnson's 3 P's of Technology Ethics:

- **Privacy—I will protect my privacy and respect the privacy of others.**

- **Property—I will protect my property and respect the property of others.**

- **a(P)propriate Use—I will use technology in constructive ways and in ways which do not break the rules of my family, religion, school, or government.**

I have also found that placing situations in which judgments about the right and wrong use of technology are made into these broad categories helps me clarify my own thinking about this huge and still expanding topic. And coming to personal understanding of ethical problems is the first step in teaching young people about them, even if that "understanding" is simply admitting confusion and resolving to study the issue.

As parents and teachers, we need to remember that it is not enough to teach our children how to use technology; we must also teach them how to use it safely and well. This book has been designed to help you do that.

National Standards

Two major sets of learning standards for students address Information and Technology Ethics:

The International Society for Technology in Education's (ISTE) "The National Educational Technology Standards for Students" <http://cnets.iste.org/>.

Social, Ethical, and Human Issues:

■ Students understand the ethical, cultural, and societal issues related to technology.

■ Students practice responsible use of technology systems, information, and software.

■ Students develop positive attitudes toward technology uses that support lifelong learning, collaboration, personal pursuits, and productivity.

American Association of School Librarians (AASL) and Association for Educational Communications and Technology's (AECT) "Information Literacy Standards for Student Learning" <http://www.ala.org/aasl/ip_nine.html>.

Social Responsibility:

■ *Standard 7:* The student who contributes positively to the learning community and to society is information literate and recognizes the importance of information to a democratic society.

■ *Standard 8:* The student who contributes positively to the learning community and to society is information literate and practices ethical behavior in regard to information and information technology.

■ *Standard 9:* The student who contributes positively to the learning community and to society is information literate and participates effectively in groups to pursue and generate information.

Now when I was a little boy growing up on the prairie, a big part of learning to shoot a gun was learning how to use it safely. I learned how to never point it at real people, how to carry it unloaded in the gun rack of the pickup, and how to hand the gun to someone else without either person getting shot. Little things like that were taught to me. Unfortunately, most computer technology comes only with how-to instructions, rarely with how-to-do-it-safely instructions.

To what extent has computer (especially Internet) use become sufficiently dangerous that instruction in its safe use should be mandatory?

_____

_____

_____

_____

_____

_____

_____

_____

_____

_____

_____

_____

_____

_____

_____

PART ONE

An Overview

Two Worlds: the Physical and the Virtual

Even very young children can quickly identify whether the behaviors in these examples are right or wrong:

- *A boy finds a magazine with sexually explicit photographs and brings it to school. He shows its contents to others in his class who become upset.*

- *A student steals a set of keys and uses them to gain access to the school office where she changes her grades and views the grades of other students.*

- *A student locates a story, recopies it in his own writing, and submits it to the teacher as his own work.*

- *A student steals a book from a local store. She says the only reason she stole it was that she did not have the money to purchase it.*

- *A student encounters an adult at the neighborhood playground who wants to start a friendship and asks the child to come home with him.*

When students start using technology, especially information technologies that consist of computers and computer networks, they start operating in a new world: a virtual world. Suddenly behaviors may not be as easily judged to be right or wrong. What would your students' responses be when given these situations?

- *A girl downloads a sexually explicit picture from a site on the Internet on a computer in the school library. Her classmates can easily view the computer screen.*

- *A student finds the teacher's password to the school's information system and uses it to change his grades and view the grades of other students.*

Finding parallels between the virtual and physical worlds can help in our understanding of online activities. The first two examples have been done for you. Discuss this concept with your students and children and see if you can complete the other examples.

PHYSICAL	VIRTUAL
Bookstore	Online bookstore
Mail	E-mail
Telephone	
	Spam
Key	
Book	
	Chatroom
	Term paper Web site
Passing notes	
Accepting ride from a stranger	
	Online file storage
Others?	

An "ethical action" is one that does not have a damaging impact on oneself, on other individuals, or on society.

■ *A student uses the copy and paste command to place large parts of an electronic encyclopedia article into an assigned paper. She turns the paper in as her own work.*

■ *A student makes a copy of a software program borrowed from another student to use on his computer at home.*

■ *A student encounters an adult in a computer chatroom who wants to start a friendship and asks the child to meet him in person.*

What's Different about "Computer Ethics?"

Computer ethics, better labeled "information technology ethics," deal with the proper use of a wide range of telecommunication and data storage devices. Ethics is the branch of philosophy that deals with moral judgments, issues of right and wrong, and determining what behaviors are humane and inhumane.

Most codes of ethical behavior describe actions that do one or more of the following as "ethical":

■ promote the general health of society

■ maintain or increase individual rights and freedoms

■ protect individuals from harm

■ treat all human beings as having an inherent value and accord those beings respect

■ uphold religious, social, cultural, and government laws and mores

A simple way of saying this is that an "ethical action" is one that does not have a damaging impact on oneself, on other individuals, or on society.

In direct and indirect ways, children begin to learn ethical values from birth. And while families and the church are assigned the primary responsibility for a child's ethical education, schools also have traditionally had the societal charge to teach and reinforce some moral values, especially those directly related to citizenship and school behaviors. Most of the ethical issues that surround technology deal with societal and school behaviors and are an appropriate and necessary part of the school curriculum.

Why do technology ethics deserve special attention? There are a variety of reasons.

Using technology to communicate and operate in a "virtual world," one that only exists within computers and computer networks, is a new phenomenon that is not always well understood by many adults who received their primary education prior to its existence.

Both fear and romance usually accompany new technologies. Our mass media has produced movies like *War Games, The Net,* and *Mission Impossible* that capitalize on the unfamiliarity many adults have of communications technologies. Movies, as well as books and television programs, often make questionably ethical actions such as breaking into secure computer systems seem heroic or sympathetic.

Our new technological capabilities require new ethical considerations.

One of the most significant reasons that computer ethics deserve special attention is because of our rather human ability to view one's actions in the intangible, virtual world of information technologies as being less serious than one's actions in the real world. Most of us, adults or children, would never contemplate walking into a computer store and shoplifting a computer program. Yet software piracy (the illegal duplication of computer programs) costs the computer business billions of dollars each year. Most of us would never pick a lock, but guessing passwords to gain access to unauthorized information is a common activity.

Information technology misuse by many people, especially the young, is viewed as a low-risk, game-like challenge.

Electronic fingerprints, footsteps, and other evidence of digital impropriety have historically

---

The terms "ethical," "safe," "moral," "appropriate," and "legal" are all used when discussing whether technology behaviors are right or wrong. While often used almost interchangeably, there are distinctions among the terms.

- Ethical use is the most generic term that applies to actions that may be considered right or wrong.

- Safe use applies to situations in which physical harm may come to a user or user's property.

- Moral use applies to situations to which religious or spiritual values apply. (Is the action good or evil?)

- Appropriate use applies to actions which may be right or wrong depending on when, where, and with whom they happen.

- Legal use applies to situations in which established laws are violated.

A single action may be unethical, unsafe, immoral, inappropriate, and illegal (such as sending a computer virus that harms data). But many acts fall more into one category and not another. The viewing of pornography arguably may be construed as immoral, but not unsafe or illegal if done by an adult in private. A student using a school computer to view sports scores is not illegal, but it could be considered inappropriate if it violates school guidelines.

How are computer technologies misrepresented in the media? What problems might these misrepresentations cause?

_____

_____

_____

_____

_____

been less detectable than physical evidence. There is a physical risk when breaking into a real office that does not exist when hacking into a computer database from one's living room or bedroom. Illegally copying a book is costly and time consuming; illegally copying a computer program can be done in seconds at very small expense. The viewed pornography on a Web site seems to disappear as soon as the browser window is closed.

Not long ago, ethical technology questions were only of interest to a very few specialists. But as the use of information technologies spreads throughout society and its importance to our national economy and to individual careers grows, *everyone* will need to make good ethical decisions when using computers. Persons involved in computer crimes acquire both their interest and skills at an early age.

Ethical Codes

Many organizations and individuals have written lists of ethical standards for technology use. One of the most widely used and easily understood sets of computer-use principles comes from the Computer Ethics Institute.

The Ten Commandments of Computer Ethics

- Thou shalt not use a computer to harm other people.
- Thou shalt not interfere with other people's computer work.
- Thou shalt not snoop around in other people's computer files.
- Thou shalt not use a computer to steal.
- Thou shalt not use a computer to bear false witness.
- Thou shalt not copy or use proprietary software for which you have not paid.

- Thou shalt not use other people's computer resources without authorization or proper compensation.

- Thou shalt not appropriate other people's intellectual output.

- Thou shalt think about the social consequences of the program you are writing or the system you are designing.

- Thou shalt always use a computer in ways that insure consideration and respect for your fellow humans.

Association for Computing Machinery's *Code of Ethics and Professional Conduct* (1993) stresses many of the same ideas as *The 10 Commandments of Computer Ethics*. Their "moral imperatives" include:

- I will contribute to society and human well-being.

- I will avoid harm to others.

- I will be honest and trustworthy.

- I will be fair and not discriminate.

- I will honor property rights including copyrights and patents.

- I will give proper credit for intellectual property.

- I will respect the privacy of others.

- I will honor confidentiality.

The ability to send unsolicited commercial messages to millions of Internet e-mail users (spamming) was not possible before there was e-mail or the Internet. Does the fact that the financial burden of unsolicited advertisements now falls on the recipient rather than the sender create the need for new rules?

Digital photography has made the manipulation of images undetectable, a nearly impossible feat with chemical photography. What obligations do communicators have to present an undoctored photograph, even if its message may not be as powerful as one that has been digitally "enhanced?"

Prior to the Internet, minors faced physical barriers of access to sexually explicit materials. What safeguards do schools, libraries, and parents need to take to keep children from freely accessing inappropriate materials? Which will better serve our children in the long run—software filtering devices or instruction and practice in making good judgments?

Intellectual property in digital format can now be duplicated with incredible ease. Do we need clearer definitions of property? Can an item that is taken without authorization, but leaves the original in place, still be considered stolen?

Can you list some other communication capabilities that did not exist prior to the Internet?

_____

_____

_____

_____

_____

_____

_____

_____

The Computer Learning Foundation has a simple set of guidelines:

Code of Responsible Computing

Respect for Privacy

I will respect others' right to privacy. I will only access, look in, or use other individuals', organizations', or companies' information on computer or through telecommunications if I have the permission of the individual, organization, or company who owns the information.

Respect for Property

I will respect others' property. I will only make changes to or delete computer programs, files, or information that belong to others, if I have been given permission to do so by the person, organization, or company who owns the program, file, or information.

Respect for Ownership

I will respect others' rights to ownership and to earn a living for their work. I will only use computer software, files, or information which I own or which I have been given permission to borrow. I will only use software programs which have been paid for or are in the public domain. I will only make a backup copy of computer programs I have purchased or written and will only use when my original programs are damaged. I will only make copies of computer files and information that I own or have written. I will only sell computer programs which I have written or have been authorized to sell by the author. I will pay the developer or publisher for any shareware programs I decide to use.

Respect for Others and the Law

I will only use computers, software, and related technologies for purposes that are beneficial to others, that are not harmful (physically, financially, or otherwise) to others or others' property, and that are within the law.

Other Codes and Guidelines

Arlene Rinaldi has written a well-respected set of Internet guidelines called "The Net: User Guidelines and Netiquette" found at <www.fau.edu/ netiquette/net/>. This more informal set of expected behaviors helps new users learn the manners and etiquette of an often-impatient online community. In her guide, newbies (inexperienced telecommunications users) learn that:

- typing in all capital letters is considered shouting and therefore rude

- sending chain letters via e-mail is improper and a waste of resources

- humor and sarcasm are easily viewed as criticism and should be used with care in electronic communications

Rinaldi isolates proper conduct for a variety of areas of telecommunication use including telnet, FTP, e-mail, discussion groups, and the World Wide Web.

Most schools now have adopted an "Acceptable Use Policy" that governs the use of the Internet and other information technologies and networks in a school. The rules in these policies often apply to both staff and students. Everyone in the school, as well as parents, needs to know and understand these policies. Some explicit rules of use from the Mankato Area Public School District's policy are listed at right and the full policy is in the Appendix of this guide.

A variety of guides should be made available to staff and students and one should either be adopted or an original set of guidelines written. While an entire school or district may wish to use a single set of guidelines, each classroom teacher needs to understand, teach, and model the guidelines. Simple, easily remembered guidelines for children are probably the best. For example:

Johnson's 3 P's of Technology Ethics:

- **Privacy—I will protect my privacy and respect the privacy of others.**

- **Property—I will protect my property and respect the property of others.**

- **a(P)propriate Use—I will use technology in constructive ways and in ways which do not break the rules of my family, religion, school, or government.**

TeenSites.com: A Field Guide to the New Digital Landscape at <www.cme.org> suggests that what teens do on the Internet "remains largely under the radar of parents, scholars, and policy makers alike."

Users are prohibited from using school district Internet resources or accounts for the following purposes:

1 To access, upload, download, or distribute pornographic, obscene, or sexually explicit material.

2 To transmit or receive obscene, abusive, or sexually explicit language.

3 To violate any local, state, or federal statute.

4 To vandalize, damage, or disable the property of another person or organization.

5 To access another person's materials, information, or files without the implied or direct permission of that person.

6 To violate copyright laws, or otherwise use another person's property without the person's prior approval or proper citation, including the downloading or exchanging of pirated software or copying software to or from any school computer.

7 Unauthorized commercial use or financial gain.

8 Internet uses shall be consistent with other school district policies as listed.

— from the Mankato Area Public Schools "Internet Acceptable Use Policy" at <www.isd77.k12.mn.us/district/isd77policies/524.htm>.

Hackers and Excuses

Educators need to be aware and understand that another, counter set of "ethical" behavior guidelines also exists; a set espoused by hackers. Being described as a "hacker" once indicated only a strong interest and ability in computer use. Popular use of the word has changed, so that now "hacking" describes gaining unauthorized access to computerized systems and data. The term "cracker" is also used, but is often used to describe a hacker who has a malicious intent. Some common hacker beliefs, stated by Deborah Johnson in _Computer Ethics_, 3rd Edition (Prentice-Hall, 2000) include:

■ All information, especially digital information, should be free and available to all people.

■ Breaking into computer systems points out security features to those who are responsible for maintaining them.

■ Hacking is a form of learning about computers and is harmless.

■ Hackers help monitor the abuse of information by the government and business.

Teachers need to know and understand these counter-culture beliefs and be able to offer reasons why they need to be questioned for their logic and ethics.

But many young people who do _not_ consider themselves "hackers" often see little harm being done by their unethical actions. Nancy Willard, in her wonderful book _Computer Ethics, Etiquette, and Safety for the 21st-Century Student_ (ISTE, 2002) suggests these "rationalizations" for student misbehavior:

■ _Finger of Blame: "He started it."_

■ _Follow the Crowd: "Everyone does it."_

■ _If I Only Had a Brain: "He told me to do it."_

■ _No Harm: "I didn't really hurt anybody."_

■ _Little Bit: "It is only a little bit wrong."_

■ _Good Intentions: "I'm doing this for a good cause."_

■ _No Consequences: "Nobody ever gets caught."_

■ _New World: "Things have changed. What used to be considered wrong is now okay."_

I might add a couple myself:

- *It's OK at Home: "My parents allow this behavior at home."*

- *Ignorance of the Law: "I didn't know it was wrong."*

- *Poor Me: "I couldn't have afforded to buy the (software, music file, etc.) anyway."*

WIIFM?

Now I don't necessarily like to take a dark view of human nature, but the reality is that most folks tend to follow rules when they know that it is in their best interest to do so. As we lay out guidelines for ethical technology behaviors, parents and teachers should keep in mind the WIIFM principle: What's In It For Me?

What is "in it" for students if they behave in an ethical manner? Some benefits include:

- If they behave legally and in keeping with school policies, they will not get in trouble with the law or school authorities.

- If they pay for software and music, they will support the authors, programmers, and musicians who can then use the profits to create more products they may enjoy.

- If they attribute sources and make their writings original, they will learn more and get the enjoyment of creation themselves.

- If they protect their privacy, they are less likely to be harassed, endangered, or spammed.

- If ethical behaviors are followed, they will feel good about themselves as students, sons or daughters, and members of a free society.

Every rule should have a benefit to the one who follows it. It just may not be very obvious or tangible.

WIIFM for these ethical actions?

- Not accessing or downloading pornographic images.
- Respecting the privacy of fellow students.
- Reporting the dangerous activities of other students.
- Not passing along hoaxes or spam.

Others?

_____

_____

_____

_____

_____

_____

_____

_____

_____

_____

_____

_____

_____

_____

_____

_____

_____

_____

POS

How did you do? Are you keeping up with your kids?

- <g> = grin
- b4 = before
- bbl = be back later
- brb = be right back
- cu = see you
- gtg = got to go
- h/o = hold o
- hw = homework
- jk = just kidding
- k = kiss
- llol = laughing out loud
- lylas = love you like a sister
- nm = never mind
- otoh = on the other hand
- rofl = rolling on the floor laughing
- sup? = what's up
- tia = thanks in advance
- tic = tongue in cheek
- ttfn = ta-ta for now
- ttyl = talk to you later
- ymmv = your mileage may vary
- w/e = whatever
- pos = parent over shoulder

Major Areas of Concern

The scope of information technology ethics is very broad. For the purposes of this book, we will be looking only at some common cases where children and young adults will need to make ethical choices or will have the unethical actions of others affect them. I have categorized the issues under the major headings of privacy, property, and appropriate use. These cases and others like them should be used to foster classroom discussion.

Feel free to use these scenarios as discussion starters with your children, with students in your classes, or with fellow professionals as part of inservice opportunities. They can be found at my Web site at <www.doug-johnson.com/ethics/> and are free to use for non-profit purposes.

Discussion Questions

1 How is ethical use by parents, teachers, and other adults the same or different from that of children and young adults?

2 What additional responsibilities do computer programmers have that computer users do not?

3 Are illegal acts always immoral? Are immoral acts always illegal?

4 Is the hacker's argument that all information should be free defensible?

PART TWO

Privacy

Τhis section presents scenarios in which young people must ask: *Does my use of the technology violate the privacy of others or am I giving information to others that I should not?*

Privacy issues are a hot-button topic as citizens become more aware of how easily technology can gather, hold, and analyze personal data and how, increasingly, their own online activities can be monitored. Students need to be aware of technology issues related to privacy so that they can protect their own privacy as well as honor the privacy of others.

Protecting One's Privacy

- Students need to understand that businesses and organizations use information to market products, and that information is often gathered electronically, both overtly and covertly. Information given to one organization may well be sold to others. All citizens should be able to articulate and control to the degree possible the amount of information a company knows about them. A company that knows a lot about an individual can use it to customize products for that person, but also can use it to manipulate him or her.

- As students use technology to communicate, they need to know that a stranger is a stranger, whether met on the playground or on the Internet. The same rules we teach children about physical strangers apply to virtual strangers as well. In conversing in chatrooms, with instant messaging programs, or through e-mail, students lose the visual clues to the other person. We know only what the other person tells about himself or herself (often much to the chagrin of those in search of romance on the Internet).

- Schools have the right to search student and employee files that are created and stored on school-owned computer hardware. Schools have search policies on lockers and book bags, and the same policy can be extended to computer storage devices.

Respecting Others' Privacy

- Because information appears on a computer screen doesn't make it public. Students who are accustomed to the public viewing of television monitors need to realize that student-created work on a computer should be treated as privately as work created in a paper journal.

- Information inadvertently left accessible does not mean that it is appropriate to access it. Forgetting to lock one's home is not the same as allowing someone to enter it. While information may be about students (such as grades), that information does not necessarily belong to them. Students certainly do not have the right to look at information about other students. One question that might be raised is: "What right do students have to check the accuracy of the data gathered about them and what would be the correct procedure for making that check?"

Discuss each of the following scenarios with your children and students.

Scenario #1

John fills out a survey form on a computer game Web page. The survey asks for his e-mail address, mailing address, and telephone number, which he fills in. In the following weeks, he receives several advertisements in the mail as well as dozens of e-mail messages about new computer games.

Questions

- Whose privacy is at risk?
- What danger or discomfort might the unethical or unwise action cause?
- Is there a parallel in the physical world to this scenario?
- What are the advantages and disadvantages of a business knowing your personal likes and dislikes?
- Can you think of other incidents that would fall into this category?

Comments

- Children and young adults need to understand that businesses and organizations use information to market products. Sometimes this information is collected without a person's permission or awareness that it is being collected, such as when Web sites use "cookies."

- Children do have some privacy under the Children's Online Privacy Protection Act, but this law applies primarily to Web sites that are targeted at children rather than regular sites that children might use. The law itself can be found at <www.kidsprivacy.com/thelaw.htm>.

Want a little bird watching out for your privacy while you are online?

Download AT&T's Privacy Bird at <www. privacybird.com/>. This small program checks accessed Web sites' privacy policies and compares them to your specified privacy preferences. The bird icon that appears in your browser's tool bar "tweets."

---

(1) IN GENERAL—It is unlawful for an operator of a Web site or online service directed to children, or any operator that has actual knowledge that it is collecting personal information from a child, to collect personal information from a child in a manner that violates the regulations prescribed under subsection (b).

— from Children's Online Privacy Protection Act of 1998 <www.kidsprivacy.com/thelaw.htm>

- Information given to one organization might be sold to others. An interesting discussion can revolve around how much a person would like a company to know about him or her. Will a company who knows a lot about me use it to customize products for me or use it to manipulate me?

- All technology users need to understand the possible ramifications of willingly or unwillingly giving others information about themselves.

Resources

- For more information about Internet privacy issues, including links to recent news stories, visit the Internet Privacy Coalition Web site at <www.privacy.org/ipc/>.

- Adams, H. *The Internet Invasion: Is Privacy at Risk?* (Follett's Professional Development Series, 2002) is a wonderful resource, especially for school library media specialists and teachers.

- A "cookie" is a small computer file stored on your computer that provides data to an Internet site about you. How can one control whether cookies are used on your browser? (For information see the United States Department of Energy's CIAC Information Bulletin I-034 Internet Cookies <http://ciac.llnl.gov/ciac/bulletins/i-034.shtml>.)

- Kids Privacy On-line at <www.kidsprivacy.com> is a great resource for parents.

Adele "meets" Frank, who shares her interest in figure skating, in an Internet chatroom. After several conversations in the following weeks, Frank asks Adele for her home telephone number and address.

Questions

- Whose privacy is at risk?

- What danger or discomfort might the unethical or unwise action cause?

- Is there a safe plan of action Adele might take to meet Frank?

- Is there a parallel in the physical world to this scenario?

- Can you think of other incidents that would fall into this category?

! The Online Enticement of Children for Sexual Acts

- People often send messages on the Internet without revealing their identity.

- Adults, some of whom may actually pose as teenagers, may want—through online contact—to meet a child for sexual purposes.

- Use of the Internet to entice, invite, or persuade a child to meet for sexual acts, or to help arrange such a meeting, is a serious offense.

— from The National Center for Missing and Exploited Children Web site

Comments

All individuals need to know that a stranger is a stranger, whether on the playground or on the Internet. The same rules we teach children about physical strangers apply to virtual strangers as well. The fact that we cannot get clues to a person from his or her physical appearance (age, dress, gender) adds to the difficulty in judging the new person.

How might Adele find out if Frank is a person whom she would like as a friend? Most groups with whom I have worked conclude that Adele needs to meet Frank in a public place accompanied by a trusted adult or group of friends (depending on her age). She could ask Frank for his phone number and call him, but some telephone services now record the number of the incoming call. In any event, Adele should not reveal any personal information to Frank until she knows that he has been representing himself fairly.

Resources

- SafeKids.com at <www.safekids.com>, produced by the Online Safety Project, has a discussion of safety issues, including privacy issues.

- The National Center for Missing and Exploited Children Internet Safety Guidelines <www.missingkids. com/cybertip>.

- FBI's Parent Guide to Internet Safety <www.fbi.gov/publications/pguide/ pguide.htm>.

Scenario #3

The principal suspects Paul of using his school e-mail account to send offensive messages to other students. He asks the school's network manager to give him copies of Paul's e-mail.

Questions

- Whose privacy is at risk?
- What danger or discomfort might the unethical or unwise action cause?
- Should students feel like "second-class citizens" because they have fewer privacy rights than adults?
- What responsibilities do parents and school officials have in making children aware of how much privacy they have?
- Is there a parallel in the physical world to this scenario?
- Can you think of other incidents that would fall into this category?

Comments

Schools (and businesses) have the right to search student and employee files that are created and stored on an organization's computer hardware. Ask your children if they know their school's search policy on lockers and book bags, and whether the same policy should be extended to computer storage devices. Recent news events have made most of us only too aware that dangerous materials can be stored in student backpacks and lockers and for the safety of all children in a school, officials need to invade an individual's privacy when there is a probable cause. Can computer files ever be considered so dangerous that safety concerns should override privacy concerns?

The _____ School District is responsible for providing safe conditions throughout the school including hallways, lockers, physical education lockers, or any other part of the school building or property. When there exists an immediate or suspected danger to the health, safety and welfare of others, school officials reserve the right to and will randomly search any and all school property.

Common language from school handbook guidelines. Does this policy extend to virtual storage spaces as well?

_____

_____

_____

_____

_____

_____

_____

_____

_____

_____

Resources

- Your school's privacy and search policies.
- Center for Democracy and Technology <www.cdt.org>.
- Electronic Frontier Foundation <www.eff.org>.

Jennie's sister needs to leave the computer to take laundry from the dryer. While she is gone, Jennie finds she has been working on an e-mail to her best friend and that her e-mail program is still open. She checks to see what sis has to say.

Questions

■ Whose privacy is at risk?

■ What danger or discomfort might the unethical or unwise action cause?

■ How do public libraries help ensure the privacy of patrons while online? Should schools do the same?

■ Is there a parallel in the physical world to this scenario?

■ Can you think of other incidents that would fall into this category?

Comments

Information inadvertently left accessible does not mean that it is appropriate to access it. Ask your child: "Is forgetting to lock one's home the same as allowing someone to enter it?"

As the writer of the e-mail at the top of the next column suggests, children may not immediately differentiate between a TV screen (public) and a computer screen (private).

Policies regarding Internet terminals in public libraries address this issue. What steps has your public library taken to help assure that its users' information needs remain private?

? "A very simple question, and one which students in our elementary schools began facing when they began using computers for word processing—the concept that all material is not public just because it appears on a screen—that is, if someone is writing using a word processor it is neither ethical nor mannerly to read the contents of that screen without first securing permission. Our third graders found this really difficult, after all that time watching a TV screen, which is open to all.

"Not a big question compared to hacking the [defense] department or posting false information on the Internet or purchasing term papers—but it was a real adjustment for our youngsters."

— from Seagraves, Hood River, Oregon. Used with permission.

Resources

■ The rules or understandings of your family.

■ Intellectual Freedom Committee of the American Library Association. Questions and Answers on Privacy and Confidentiality <www.ala.org/alaorg/oif/privacyqanda.html>.

Ms. West, Terry's teacher, needs to leave the room to take care of an emergency. While she is gone, Terry finds that Ms. West had been working on student progress reports and that her grading program is still open. He checks to see what grade he is getting and finds the grades for several other students.

Questions

- Whose privacy is at risk?

- What danger or discomfort might the unethical or unwise action cause?

- What efforts might a school take to prevent such occurrences?

- What do teachers need to know about student privacy issues?

- Is there a parallel in the physical world to this scenario?

- Can you think of other incidents that would fall into this category?

Comments

While information may be about a child (such as grades), that information does not necessarily belong to the child. And children certainly do not have the right to look at information about others. One question that might be raised is: "What right do I, as a student, have to check the accuracy of the data gathered about me, and what would be the correct procedure for making that check?"

Teachers also have a responsibility for taking measures that will secure the privacy of their students. The profession has been well-trained not to leave a paper gradebook open or unattended. Do all teachers understand the importance of

? **What can teachers do to help create a "low temptation" environment in their classroom?**

_____

_____

_____

_____

_____

_____

_____

_____

_____

_____

_____

_____

closing electronic gradebook programs and logging off networks when the computer is not being used?

Schools are increasingly implementing programs that allow parents Web access to their students' school data including grades, attendance records, gradebook entries, and discipline data. What are the security and privacy issues that such programs create?

Resources

- Johnson, D. "Teacher Webpages That Build Parent Partnerships." (*MultiMedia Schools*, September 2000) <www.infotoday.com/MMSchools/sep00/johnson.htm>.

Alfreda received an unsolicited e-mail in her student account for a product. Included in the e-mail was an e-mail address she could respond to if she did not wish to receive any additional e-mail from this company. After replying, the volume of spam in her account increased dramatically.

? What advice can you offer e-mail users to reduce the amount of unsolicited e-mail they receive? How do you respond to an e-mail user who begins to receive spam for unwanted or even unsavory products?

Questions

- Whose privacy is at risk?

- What danger or discomfort might the unethical or unwise action cause?

- How serious is spam? Is it merely an annoyance or does it have a genuine cost to the individual or organization?

- Is there a parallel in the physical world to this scenario?

- Can you think of other incidents that would fall into this category?

Comments

Of growing concern to many e-mail users is the amount of unsolicited e-mail (spam) cluttering their in-boxes.

Is harm caused by spam? Like telephone marketing, it seems victimless, however:

- It wastes resources of employees and students (time spent removing spam), bandwidth, and mail server storage space.

- It causes personal embarrassment for the recipients of less savory, unsolicited e-mail. Many teachers and students have been quite upset about getting spam that advertises pornography (even child pornography), Viagra and its ilk, and other products that seem terribly personal. (I always feel bad about getting spam for hair restorer—how do *they* know about my bald spot?)

- A good deal of spam is for investment and money-making schemes that are obviously fraudulent. The SEC has even put out a site about this issue. (See Property Scenario #9.) The less informed and financially desperate are likely prey for this kind of spam.

There are no easy answers to eliminating or reducing spam. Anyone who responds to a Web site or an e-mail with a poor privacy policy; anyone who has an e-mail address on a Web site; or anyone who participates in chatrooms is a target for spammers. Some suggestions that are commonly offered:

- Do not respond to spam, even when the e-mail provides an address for removing one from the list.

- Use a Yahoo or Hotmail e-mail address when transacting business on the Web that can be changed if the spam begins to build.

- Check to see if your e-mail software allows you to build a filter for common terms in spam (Viagra, mortgage, sexy, etc.).

- Choose an Internet provider that offers a spam filtering service.

- Check to see if your district can add a spam filter to its firewall or e-mail server.

Resources

- Do it yourself: Stop junk mail, e-mail, and phone calls at <www.obviously.com/junkmail>.

Scenario #7

Mr. Black, the school library media specialist, publicly posts lists of overdue materials on the school Intranet. The lists include student names and titles of the materials. Clarice is upset by this policy and asks the principal how it can be changed.

Questions

- Whose privacy is at risk?
- What danger or discomfort might the unethical or unwise action cause?
- Is there a parallel in the physical world to this scenario?
- What alternatives are there to posting the names and overdue material titles to the Intranet?
- What is Mr. Black's ethical responsibility when he is asked for the titles of materials Clarice may have checked out this past year by
  - ▶ her parents?
  - ▶ school administrators or teachers?
  - ▶ law enforcement officials?

Can you think of other incidents that would fall into this category?

Comments

Adults need to understand the data privacy rights of children. Librarians have long supported these rights. The American Library Association's Code of Ethics clearly states: "We protect each library user's right to privacy and confidentiality with respect to information sought or received and resources consulted, borrowed, acquired, or transmitted."

This had not been an uncontentious issue. Parents, school officials, and law enforcement officials request data about children's library resources use for a variety of reasons. As the use of digital resources continues to increase, so will questions about what access adults should have to information about what young people use.

School staff, especially school librarians, when making decisions about student privacy issues, should ask themselves the following questions when asked for student information:

- What are my school's policies and state and federal laws regarding the confidentiality of student information? Have I consulted with and can I expect support from my administration regarding decisions I make regarding student privacy? Is there recourse to the school's legal counsel regarding difficult or contentious issues?
- What is the legitimate custodial responsibility of the person or group asking for information about a student?
- How accurately and specifically can I provide that information?
- By providing such information is there a reasonable chance the information may prevent some harm to either the individual or to others in the school or community?
- Is there a legitimate pedagogical reason to share student information with a teacher? Am I sharing information about materials that students are using for curricular purposes or for personal use?
- Have I clearly stated to my students what the library guidelines are on the release of personal information? If the computers in the library are or can be remotely monitored, is there a clear statement of that fact readily posted?
- If student activity on a computer is logged, are students aware of this record, how long the log is kept, how the log may be used, and by whom?

Resources

- American Library Association's "Code of Ethics" <www.ala.org/alaorg/oif/ ethics.html>.
- American Library Association's "Privacy: An Interpretation of the Library Bill of Rights" <www.ala.org/alaorg/oif/privacyinterpretation. html>.

Scenario #8

Joel shared his password for his e-mail network access account with his buddy Lyle. He has found that several documents are missing from his online storage space.

Questions

- Whose privacy is at risk?

- What danger or discomfort might the unethical or unwise action cause?

- How does one create an "unguessable" password?

- Is there a parallel in the physical world to this scenario?

- Can you think of other incidents that would fall into this category?

Comments

I am continually amazed at how lightly people (including myself, I suppose) treat the confidentiality of their passwords. Students need to understand the risk of sharing passwords, why passwords should not be written down, the wisdom of changing their passwords on a regular basis, how to create a less "guessable" password, and proper log-out procedures from networked computers. Oh, and so should adults.

Whenever the software allows it, we force a required change of password on a regular (60-day) basis. Not exactly popular with everyone, but it is important.

Stealing passwords is illegal. It is a violation of the Federal Law, 18 USC 1029.

— from *Internet & Computer Ethics for Kids*. Interpact Press, 2001.

Resources

- Lockdown Password FAQ <www. lockdown. co.uk/security/password_faq.php>.

What advice can you give to your children or students about protecting their passwords?

_____

_____

_____

_____

_____

_____

_____

_____

_____

_____

_____

_____

_____

Scenario #9

While the teacher was out of the room, Trixie decided to visit a site that she knew violated the school and classroom rules. The next day, the teacher brought Trixie and her parents in for a conference. A program on the computer she was using logged the Internet sites she visited. Trixie felt her privacy had been violated.

Questions

- Whose privacy is at risk?

- What danger or discomfort might the unethical or unwise action cause?

- If a school or family decides to use software to monitor computer use remotely, is there an ethical responsibility to inform computer users of that decision?

- Is there a parallel in the physical world to this scenario?

- Can you think of other incidents that would fall into this category?

Comments

Schools and households have a number of remote monitoring systems available to them. Schools are increasingly asking students to log on to the network and special software then records each action a student takes. Computer technicians and others can remotely observe student workstations using products like *Apple Network Administrator's Toolkit* or *PCAnywhere*. Recording software is being aggressively marketed to homes.

Remote monitoring of computer use is becoming a reality in not just schools, but in the business world as well. Big Brother has arrived. It just took him a few more years than Orwell predicted.

? In the book *The Good, the Bad & the Difference: How to Tell Right from Wrong in Everyday Situations* (Doubleday, 2002), Randy Cohen questions the rights of institutions to monitor employee computer use. He makes the analogy that just because the company owns the bathrooms, that doesn't give it the right to install video cameras there. How good is Cohen's comparison?

_____

_____

_____

_____

_____

_____

_____

_____

_____

_____

_____

_____

_____

_____

_____

Resources

- Head, S. "Big Brother in a Black Box." (*Civilization*, August–September, 1999)

Ike and Tina created a Web page to meet the requirements of a school assignment. On the Web page they included their pictures and e-mail addresses in hopes of getting feedback on their page.

Questions

- Whose privacy is at risk?

- What danger or discomfort might the unethical or unwise action cause?

- Should young writers be encouraged to publish writings to the Web?

- Is there a parallel in the physical world to this scenario?

- Can you think of other incidents that would fall into this category?

Comments

Research on writing has shown that students are more conscientious when they know they have an audience that will comment and respond. Posting student writing to the Web is a means of providing this audience.

Schools need to develop privacy policies that help protect students from "responses" from irresponsible and possibly dangerous people. By not including photographs and listing only the e-mail address of a teacher who can relay responses back to the student authors, young people are protected.

" Student Safeguards

While district policies and related statutes pertaining to "directory information" may allow the release of some personal data about students, we have chosen to establish the following guidelines:

- Documents shall include only the first name of the student.

- Documents shall not include a student's home phone number or address or the names of other family members or friends.

- Published e-mail addresses shall be restricted to those of staff members.

- Decisions on publishing student pictures (digitized or video) and audio clips are based on the supervising teacher's judgment and signed permission of the student and parent or guardian.

- No student work shall be published without permission of the student and parent or guardian.

— from the Mankato Area Schools "World Wide Web Page Creation Guidelines" <www.isd77.k12.mn.us/webguide.php>

Resources

- Web page guidelines in the Appendix to this guide.

- Education Queensland (Australia) Publishing at <education.qld.gov.au/publication/> has a fine set of guidelines for Web publishing for schools.

Anne has a credit card with the permission of her parents. She finds a music CD that is not available locally on a Web site. She fills in the online order form with her name, address, telephone number, and credit card account number and hits the "submit" button.

Questions

- Whose privacy is at risk?

- What danger or discomfort might the unethical or unwise action cause?

- Is making a credit card purchase using a Web site riskier than making a purchase in a store? Over the phone? By mail?

- Is there a parallel in the physical world to this scenario?

- Can you think of other incidents that would fall into this category?

Comments

Identity theft is a frightening and increasingly common phenomenon. Criminals do this by using another's name, Social Security number, credit card number, or some other piece of personal information for their own use. In short, identity theft occurs when someone appropriates another's personal information without that person's knowledge to commit fraud or theft. Specific data on the prevalence of identity theft as collected by the Government Accounting Office can be found at <www.consumer.gov/idtheft/reports.htm>.

How real is the risk of sharing personal data online? Should purchases be made online? Two factors need to be considered:

- one's own comfort with and understanding of the kinds of risks association with online transactions

- the ability to discern the reliability and security of companies who offer online commerce

---

Identity theft may be as old as Internet commerce, but crooks still come up with new ways to trick unsuspecting people into giving out sensitive personal information like credit card or Social Security numbers.

Bank of America Scam

The scam: Someone posing as a Bank of America associate sent out a fraudulent e-mail asking BoA customers to enter personal financial information on a fake Web site posing as a BoA Web site. Fortunately, the bank became aware of this e-mail within hours, and authorities quickly shut the scam site down.

The truth: Like most banks, BoA does not contact customers out of the blue to verify personal financial information. You may be asked to verify such information if you call the bank about your banking matters.

What to do: If someone—anyone—contacts you by phone or e-mail, asking you for sensitive personal information, be very wary. Contact the company they claim to represent directly, using a phone number or e-mail address from the company's Web site, and confirm the story.

Never be in a rush to give out your information until you know it's safe.

— from Internet ScamBusters #50, May 13, 2002

Students need to made aware of ways they can minimize the risk of identify theft.

Resources

- ID Theft: the U.S. government's central Web site for information about identity theft at <www.consumer.gov/idtheft/>.

- Gralla, P. *The Complete Idiot's Guide to Protecting Your Children Online*. Que, 2000.

In Sun-Kim's house the computer with Internet access is in the family room. Sun-Kim has been lobbying her mother to let her have a computer with Internet access in her room since her younger brothers often make it difficult for her to concentrate while she is online.

Questions

- Whose privacy is at risk?
- What danger or discomfort might the unethical or unwise action cause?
- How can adults best ensure that children use online resources appropriately? How effective:
  - ▶ is a physical presence?
  - ▶ are filters?
  - ▶ are remote monitoring systems?
  - ▶ is logging software?
- Is there a parallel in the physical world to this scenario?
- Can you think of other incidents that would fall into this category?

Comments

Parents have some tough choices to make. Among them is how much access to give their children to technologies that can be used in both productive and unproductive (or even dangerous) ways by their children. Parents have been advised forever about the importance of establishing a quiet area in which their children can study. This now needs to be balanced with the importance of monitoring children's activity while online.

Families have different rules about what their children should be able to have in their rooms: televisions, telephones, food, girlfriends, boyfriends, etc. Computers and the Internet now need to be considered as well.

> "It is critical that our children have your guidance as they learn to use the Internet. Although children can use the Internet to tap in to the Library of Congress or download pictures from the surface of Mars, not all of the material on the Internet is appropriate for children. As a parent, you can guide and teach your child in a way that no one else can. You can make sure that your child's experience on the Internet is safe, educational, and enjoyable."

— from "Message To Parents About The Internet" by President Clinton <www.kidsource.com/kidsource/content4/internet_1.morph.html>

Resources

- A simple search on "parents guide to internet use" in Google or another Internet search engine will result in a large number of guides written by responsible organizations.

- See "What Homes Need to Do to Teach and Encourage Ethical Behaviors" in this book.

Discussion Questions

1 When is shared data harmful? When is it helpful? Can some kinds of shared data be helpful to society, but harmful to an individual?

2 What steps can individuals, adult and child, take to protect their privacy?

3 Does the school or government have a role in assuring its citizens' data privacy?

4 How available should this information about your children be to others?
- Their school records.
- The last three books they read or last three computer programs they purchased.
- The sites they visit on the World Wide Web.
- Their favorite foods and fashions.

5 How can we help students understand the value of respecting the privacy of others?

PART THREE

Property

This section presents scenarios in which young people must ask: *Do my actions respect the property of others and am I taking steps to keep my property safe?*

Property issues, especially those regarding intellectual property, have come to the forefront of ethics discussions. As noted earlier in this guide, the ease with which property can be copied has led to greater instances of piracy, plagiarism, and even disdain for copyright laws as evidenced in the rampant use of Napster-like music acquisition. Like privacy, students need to understand that property is a two-sided issue: they need to respect the property of others as well as protect their own property from the abuses of others.

Respecting the Property of Others

■ Students need to know that computer software is protected by copyright law. It is unlawful, as well as unethical, to make copies of computer programs without permission or payment to the producer of those programs. It also needs to be understood that when purchasing software, one is usually only purchasing the right to use the software. The ownership of the code that comprises the program stays with the producer. This means that one cannot alter the program and that there may be restrictions on reselling it. The vast majority of software licenses require that one copy of a program be purchased for each computer on which it is to be run. The inability to pay for software is not a justification for illegal copying.

■ Software falls into three main types: freeware (that which can be used indefinitely without payment); shareware (that which can be used for a trial period and then must either be erased or purchased); and commercial software (that which must be purchased before use). Understanding the concept of shareware helps students understand why purchasing software benefits them. The profits that software producers make are partially used to fund the development of more software. If the profit motive is lost from software creation, less software and fewer improvements are likely to be made.

- Plagiarism is easier than ever, thanks to the computer. Students need to understand when and how to cite information from a broad range of print, electronic, and primary sources. Academic work is increasingly available for sale or download from the Internet. Online services now offer help in writing "personal" essays requested for college admissions offices.

- Both hacking and creating viruses are property offenses because they cause damage or misuse technology resources such as bandwidth.

- Students need to learn to treat intellectual property the same way they would treat physical property and that the theft or destruction of such property is unethical (and unlawful). Deleting a file or erasing a disk constitutes the destruction of property even though the magnetic medium of the hard drive or the plastic case of the computer disk is left intact.

- Deliberate waste of school materials through excessive printing is not uncommon. Students need to understand that it is wrong to waste finite resources. Like vandalism, students need to understand that everyone is affected by such activities.

Protecting One's Own Property

- Students need to know about the unethical practices of others and how to protect themselves from those practices.

- Computer viruses, often infecting a computer through downloading software from the Internet, can be detected and destroyed by virus protection programs. Students need to know how to find, install, and use these programs.

- Investment, health, and employment scams are rampant on the Internet.

- Students need to know that their own original work is protected by copyright laws and that they have a right to give or not give permission for others to use it.

- All technology users need to know that passwords must be kept confidential to prevent unauthorized access to a student's data (and to ensure privacy).

- All citizens (including students) have the ethical responsibility to report wrongdoing, including destruction of property. While there are many reasons why students are reluctant to do so, as adults we need to express our beliefs that reporting unethical or criminal behavior serves a social purpose. Younger students often believe that school property is owned by the teachers and administrators and are surprised to learn that it is their parents' taxes or fees that pay for vandalized or stolen school resources.

Discuss each of the following scenarios with your children and students.

Scenario #1

Jerry borrows Ben's game disks for Monster Truck Rally II *and installs them on his home computer. He says he will erase the game if he does not like it or will buy the game for himself if he likes it.*

Questions

- What is the property?

- Who is its owner?

- What danger or discomfort might the unethical action cause?

- Is there a parallel in the physical world to this scenario?

- Is digital media more likely to be unlawfully copied than physical media (books, videotapes, etc.)? Why?

- Can you think of other incidents that would fall into this category?

Comments

Students need to know that computer software is protected by copyright law. It is unlawful, as well as unethical, to make copies of computer programs without permission or payment of the producers of those programs. It also needs to be understood that when purchasing software, one usually only purchases the right to use the software. The ownership of the code that comprises the program stays with the producer and the rights to alter or resell the software may be restricted. The vast majority of software licenses require that one copy of a program be purchased for each computer on which it is to be run. And no, the inability to pay for software is not a justification for illegal copying anymore than the inability to pay for a book is any justification for shoplifting it from a bookstore.

Resources

- The Software & Industry Information Association (formerly the Software Publishers Association) at <www.spa.org> has an interesting "anti-piracy" page and FAQ (list of frequently asked questions).

- The online article "The Napster Cantata" by M. E. Kabay at <networking. earthweb.com/netsysm/article/ 0,,12089_625221,00.html> does a good job of offering counter arguments to the rationalizations of software pirates in language students can understand. For example: "We won't get caught. So what? That's irrelevant to whether they ought to be doing it. Being caught has no bearing on whether an act is moral or legal: What do you think hit-and-run accidents are all about? Knocking someone over with your car is OK as long as you don't get caught? Doing bad things gets to be a habit regardless of whether anyone finds out about it. And companies that tolerate any kind of illegality by their employees while on company time or on company systems are opening themselves up to blackmail, denunciation, and lawsuits."

"As children have access to computers earlier and earlier in their educational careers, experts in piracy, hacking, and other forms of Internet mischief say that any effort to tackle the illicit trade in digital goods—including video games, computer software, music, and even movies—should be looking at a younger crowd.

" 'By the time we get them, they already believe it's right,' said David J. Farber, a professor of computer science at the University of Pennsylvania."

— from *The New York Times,* Tuesday, December 25, 2001

Scenario #2

Betty downloads a solitaire card game that is "shareware" from the Internet. It can be legally used for 30 days and then Betty must either delete it from her computer or send its author a fee. Betty has been using the game for 30 days.

Questions

- What is the property?

- Who is its owner?

- What danger or discomfort might the unethical action cause?

- What is the advantage to the user for paying for shareware?

- Is there a parallel in the physical world to this scenario?

- Can you think of other incidents that would fall into this category?

> **?** "Why do authors use shareware to distribute their product? Basically, it's efficient. Costs are generally less than for software sold through traditional channels. Lower operating costs mean shareware authors can concentrate on writing great programs, while often charging users less. Shareware also allows authors to retain complete control. Microsoft and Netscape are just two software companies that have recognized benefits of 'try-before-you-buy' distribution."
>
> — from the Association of Shareware Professionals

Comments

Software falls into three main types: free-ware (that which can be used without payment indefinitely); shareware (that which can be use for a trial period and then must either be erased or purchased); and commercial software (that which must be purchased before use).

Understanding the concept of shareware helps students understand why purchasing software benefits them. The profits that software producers make are partially used to fund the development of more software. If the profit motive is lost from software creation, less software and fewer improvements are likely to be made.

One additional WIIFM (What's In It For Me) is that a licensed version of the shareware product often contains additional features and it may drop annoying reminders to register the shareware.

Students need to learn to read the licensing agreement of any piece of software.

Resources

- Association of Shareware Professionals at <www.asp-shareware.org/> has a good FAQ (list of frequently asked questions) for shareware users.

Scenario #3

Cindy finds some good information about plant growth nutrients for her science fair project on a CD-ROM reference title that came with her home computer. She uses the copy function of the computer to take an entire paragraph from the CD-ROM article and pastes it directly into her report. She also forgets to write down the title of the article and the CD-ROM from which it was taken. When she writes her report, she does not cite the source in her bibliography.

Questions

- What is the property?

- Who is its owner?

- What danger or discomfort might the unethical action cause?

- Is most plagiarism deliberate or due to a lack of understanding?

- Is there a parallel in the physical world to this scenario?

- Can you think of other incidents that would fall into this category?

"Another big issue is citing sources from Web pages. It is so easy to cut and paste and forget to include the source. It was always difficult going back and finding information for books when one forgot to write the citation, but on the Internet it's even more of a challenge. Without bookmarks it's often impossible to relocate a site."

—from Roz Goodman, Media Specialist, Dillingham, Arkansas. Reprinted with permission.

? What are some other effective techniques students can use to record sources of information and remember direct quotations?

Comments

Plagiarism is easier than ever, thanks to the computer. Students need to understand when and how to cite sources in both print and electronic formats. Some plagiarism is of course deliberate, but much of it stems from a lack of understanding of what and when to cite. Direct, repeated instruction by library media specialists and teachers needs to be done as a part of each project requiring research. Parents, when proofing their children's writing, should be asking if proper credit has been given for others' work.

Resources

- An interesting discussion of one such incident can be found at: "Is It Plagiarism?" at <www.doug-johnson.com/dougwri/isit.html>.

- The Purdue Online Writing Laboratory (OWL) has excellent guidelines on when citation is necessary at <http://owl.english.purdue.edu/handouts/research/r_plagiar.html>.

Scenario #4

Albert finds a site on the Internet that is a repository of old term papers. He downloads one on ancient Greece, changes the title, and submits it as his own.

Questions

- What is the property?

- Who is its owner?

- What danger or discomfort might the unethical action cause?

- How might teachers change assignments to make them less likely to be found on term paper Internet sites?

- Is there a parallel in the physical world to this scenario?

- Can you think of other incidents that would fall into this category?

Comments

Academic work is increasingly available for sale or download from the Internet from a number of sites. Schools Sucks at <www. schoolsucks.com> is probably one of the oldest and best known. Online services now offer help in writing "personal" essays requested for college

From: info@getpapers.net
Sent: Wednesday, February 27, 2002
    3:56 AM
To: student@isd77.k12.mn.us
Subject: Essays

Dear Student!

GetPapers.net is proud to share with you its online database of 35,000+ high-quality essays all collected from top U.S. universities. Please visit us at http://www.GetPapers.net!

This is a one-time mailing.
Have a nice day!

> "Tamara Ballou, who is helping implement an honor code at her Falls Church, Virginia high school, said that it is not uncommon for teachers and students to disagree on what constitutes academic dishonesty.
>
> " 'We took a long time to define cheating,' she said, noting that many kids felt it was acceptable to copy homework from each other or off the Internet if the assignment was perceived as 'busy work.' "
>
> —from Dustin Goot, "Thin Line Splits Cheating, Smarts." *WiredNews*, September 10, 2002 <www.wired.com/news/school/0,1383,54963,00. html>.

admissions offices. How are such services like or unlike ghostwritten biographies and speeches of celebrities and politicians?

One way teachers can help defeat the use of such sites is to ask for papers that call for original thoughts and conclusions. Does your child's teacher ask for papers that call for creativity?

Resources

- A discussion of this issue can be found in "Copy, Cut, Plagiarize," *Technology Connection,* January 1996 <www.doug-johnson.com/dougwri/cut.html>.

- Web sites like Turnitin at <turnitin.com> will check a suspect paper for copied content. Such sites charge a fee after a limited trial period.

- When a suspect sentence or phrase, placed in quotes, is typed into a search engine like <google.com>, the source of that sentence may be displayed.

- See the section "Plagiarism-Proofing Assignments" in this guide.

Scenario #5

Fahad is upset with his friend George. He finds the data disk on which George has been storing his essays and erases it.

Questions

- What is the property?

- Who is its owner?

- What danger or discomfort might the unethical action cause?

- Is there a parallel in the physical world to this scenario?

- How can you help students or children reliably create and store backup copies of important work?

- Can you think of other incidents that would fall into this category?

Comments

Does deleting a file or erasing a disk constitute the destruction of property? After all the magnetic medium of the hard drive or the plastic case of the computer disk is left intact. All that has changed is the polarization of some magnetic particles bonded to a circle of plastic. Students need to learn to treat intellectual property, existing only in virtual spaces, the same way they would treat physical property and that the theft or destruction of such property is unethical (and unlawful).

Digital information can also be accidentally destroyed or lost. In my experience, few words associated with technology are as heartbreaking as: "This disk is damaged and can't be read. It has the only copy of the assignment I've been working on for the past month." (And students aren't the only ones I've heard this from.) We need to make sure that the ability to make backup copies of original data is available for both students and staff.

Resources

- There are a number of free online file storage sites on the Web. One example is Yahoo! Briefcase at <briefcase.yahoo.com>. Online storage, whether provided by the school, the student's family, or by a commercial Web site, is a good way to move files from the school to home and back. It can also help overcome compatibility conflicts (Window/Macintosh) when the home and school don't use the same computer platform.

The ~~dog~~ computer ate my homework.

A computer malfunction is the newest excuse for not completing work on time. How can we separate the genuine problems from the creative excuses?

- Students should make print copies of drafts of their work as the ultimate backup. Without at least some evidence of previous work like a hard copy, it is reasonable to doubt the "computer ate my homework" excuse.

- Other ideas?

Lucy uses the family computer to download a program from the Internet that has instructions on how to make paper airplanes. After using the program, the computer does not seem to work very well, crashing often and randomly destroying files. Lucy thinks she might have downloaded a virus along with the paper airplane program.

Questions

- What is the property?

- Who is its owner?

- What danger or discomfort might the unethical action cause?

- Is there a parallel in the physical world to this scenario?

- Can you think of other incidents that would fall into this category?

Doug,

Last night my daughter was on her computer at home and a hacker came on. Her screen went blank and she was just typing on a dark background. He told her he had taken everything. She finally got it back. Is there anything you can do when someone hacks into your computer at home like that? He even said he could see her even though her camera was turned off. Is that a possibility? She was really scared. She said that if he hadn't returned her stuff that we would have had to buy a new computer. Is that right? I'm so computer illiterate. Please shed some light. Where can I report it? The guy claimed to be from the U.K. He was Jack the Fecker. HELP!

Becky

—from personal e-mail, May 2002

Comments

Students need to know about the unethical practices of others and how to protect themselves from those practices. Computer viruses, often infecting a computer through downloading software from the Internet or opening e-mail attachments, can be detected and destroyed by virus protection programs. Students need to know how to find, install, update, and use these programs.

Adults can install management programs on computers that will not allow unauthorized users to install software or run applications. Schools should consider using such software to reduce both the spread of viruses and the time needed to maintain computer operating systems.

As more families gain broadband access (ISDN lines, cable modems, wireless connectivity), there will be a growing need for a firewall that will prevent hackers from gaining access to home computers becomes critical. (See e-mail on this page.) While WindowsXP has built-in firewall features, it may be best to work with a security professional to make sure it is set up correctly.

Resources

- One resource that gives recent information about computer viruses is F-Secure Corporation at <www.datafellows.com/virus-info/>.

- A sample software installation policy statement can be found at <www.ncrel.org/tplan/handbook/toolkt12.htm>.

Henry's friend Hank has discovered the password to the school's student information system. Because Hank feels a teacher has unfairly given him a poor grade, he plans to create a "bomb," which will erase all the information on the office computer.

Questions

- What is the property?

- Who is its owner?

- What danger or discomfort might the unethical action cause?

- What's the WIIFM (What's In It For Me?) in this case?

- Is there a parallel in the physical world to this scenario?

- Can you think of other incidents that would fall into this category?

> "Hackers are not bad people.
>
> "In fact, 99+% of hackers do a lot of good. They are programmers, engineers, and technicians who design software, build products, and keep millions of computer networks running.
>
> "It's the other 1% who give hacking a bad name. Just like real life."
>
> —from Winn Schwartau at <www.NiceKids.net>

Comments

Citizens (including students) have the ethical responsibility for reporting wrongdoing, including destruction of property. And while there are lots of reasons why students are reluctant to do so, as adults, we need to express our beliefs that reporting unethical or criminal behavior serves a social purpose. Younger students often believe that school property is owned by the teachers and administrators, and are surprised to learn that it is their parents' taxes or fees that must be used to pay for vandalized or stolen school resources.

I have heard sad stories of students, who when in high school got in trouble for hacking, later finding difficulty getting security clearance in the military. A cautionary tale for students, perhaps?

Resources

- The book *Internet & Computer Ethics for Kids* by Winn Schwartau (Impact Press, 2001) is a great introduction to hacker-type misuse of information technologies. Do you know what "phreaking" is or who a "black hat" might be?

- Deborah Johnson's book *Computer Ethics* (Prentice-Hall, 2000) also has an intelligent discussion of the hacker point of view.

Brady has been taking advantage of a Napster-like, peer-to-peer service to download all his favorite songs, save them on his hard drive, and load them to his MP3 player. He can cite articles that show the sales of music CDs have actually risen as a result of music "swapping" on the Internet.

Questions

- What is the property?

- Who is its owner?

- What danger or discomfort might the unethical action cause?

- At what point does the widespread refusal to obey a law make the law irrelevant? (Think "blue laws" of years past.)

- Is there an ethical difference between using "swapped" music for personal use and burning CDs of music for giving or selling to others?

- Is there a parallel in the physical world to this scenario?

- Can you think of other incidents that would fall into this category?

Comments

Accessing music and movies over the Internet using peer-to-peer services is common practice among many young people. Despite the closure of Napster, a variety of smaller, lower-profile services still exist.

Recording companies have been slow to respond with alternative electronic music distribution systems. But even if the current systems are seen as unfair to young computer users, copyright laws need to be followed.

? "Chief among the new rules is that 'content is free.' While not all content will be free, the new economic dynamic will operate as if it were. In the world of the Net, content (including software) will serve as advertising for services such as support, aggregation, filtering, assembly, and integration of content modules, or training of customers in their use. Intellectual property that can be copied easily likely will be copied. It will be copied so easily and efficiently that much of it will be distributed free in order to attract attention or create desire for follow-up services that can be charged for.

"What should content makers do in such an inverted world? The likely best course for content providers is to exploit that situation, to distribute intellectual property free in order to sell services and relationships."

—from Ester Dyson

Resources

These are two seminal articles about the impact of the Internet on intellectual property rights that are well worth reading:

- John Perry Barlow, "The Economy of Ideas: A framework for patents and copyrights in the Digital Age." *Wired*, Mar 1994 <www.wired.com/wired/archive/2.03/economy.ideas.html>

- Ester Dyson, "Intellectual Value." *Wired*, July 1995 <www.wired.com/wired/archive/3.07/dyson.html>

Sara has begun working and has some money she would like to invest. She receives an e-mail that promises a 500% return on her investment. She sends the company a check for $200.

Questions

- What is the property?
- Who is its owner?
- What danger or discomfort might the unethical action cause?
- Is there a parallel in the physical world to this scenario?
- Can you think of other incidents that would fall into this category?

Comments

The scam artists are out in full force, preying on both adults and children. Whether on the Internet, on the phone, or on paper, if it looks too good to be true, it is. Students need to learn how to check the reliability of investment opportunities. (Big words coming from a WorldCom stockholder, huh?)

Resources

- Scambusters at <www.scambusters.org/>. At the site, one can subscribe to a very good electronic newsletter that describes the latest Internet scams.

The Securities and Exchange Commission (SEC) published a "fake" press release and Web site in February of 2002 to alert investors and others to read, question, and apply critical information skills when analyzing information.

Here are the URLs:

- "SEC uses fake site to warn investors" at <news.com.com/2100-1023-823578.html>.
- The fake press release as it ran on PR Newswire at <http://library.northernlight.com/FC20020125750000051.html>.
- The fake "McWhortle Enterprises" Web site at <www.mcwhortle.com>.

Scenario #10

Raul is creating a videotape for his History Day project. As background music he is using Billy Joel's song "We Didn't Start the Fire" that he has digitized from a CD he owns. The song works well for his exploration of the causes of global conflict. The projects will compete initially within his school and winners will advance to regional, public competitions.

Questions

- What is the property?

- Who is its owner?

- What danger or discomfort might the unethical action cause?

- Is there a parallel in the physical world to this scenario?

- Can you think of other incidents that would fall into this category?

Comments

Fair use is murky waters. Section 107 of the Copyright Act lists four fair use factors which should be considered when determining whether a use is a "fair use":

- Is the purpose commercial or for nonprofit educational purposes?

- What is the nature of the copyrighted work?

- How much of the work is to be used in relation to the copyrighted work as a whole?

- What might the effect of the use be on the potential market for or value of the copyrighted work?

    Generally students may use a portion of copyrighted materials to meet educational goals in classes and in portfolios if the source is properly cited.

Resources

- Carol Simpson's *Copyright for Schools* (Linworth) is probably the most understandable book on issues of copyright, including fair use, now available. Be sure you have the latest edition.

- Jefferson County (Colorado) copyright chart and guidelines <http://jeffcoweb.jeffco.k12.co.us/plmc/copyright.html>.

- CONFU Fair Use Guidelines for Educational Media <www.utsystem.edu/OGC/IntellectualProperty/ccmcguid.htm>.

> " "I have made teaching citation techniques and avoiding plagiarism my mission in life. One of the teachers I am working with does not think either of us is making any headway with the basic underlying attitudes that our kids have about it. They just do not seem to feel that there is anything unethical about it. We are working with 11th graders on a long-term project. Their works cited lists are in. They have done a good job with that because a good chunk of their grade depended on it—and I was grading it, so they knew someone who knows their way around the Internet would be grading them not only for format, but to make sure the sites were reputable. However—they were very resistant to the whole presentation we made, insisting that no college professor was ever going to be checking their sources in any great detail. No one cares about the quality of the sources used. As long as they used a lot of sources and put together a lot of support for their thesis from a lot of different sources, no one would ever catch them anyway. Etc. etc. etc. Their papers have not been turned in yet—so checking for possible plagiarism is still ahead of us."

—from Jacquie Henry, Librarian, Gananda Middle-High School, Walworth, New York 14568. From LM_Net April 2002. Used with permission.

Barry is very careful about not plagiarizing. When using information from the online encyclopedia, he is careful about changing at least a few words in each sentence.

Questions

- What is the property?

- Who is its owner?

- What danger or discomfort might the unethical action cause?

- Is there a parallel in the physical world to this scenario?

- Can you think of other incidents that would fall into this category?

Comments

Students need to understand the difference between direct plagiarism, paraphrasing, and writing original work. Apparently some nationally recognized authors do as well!

Resources

- An online example of a practice activity can be found at Cody's Science Education Zone at <http://ousd.k12.ca.us/~codypren/antidote.html>.

- One interesting site is at Indiana University Bloomington at <www.indiana.edu/~wts/wts/plagiarism.html>. It gives examples of acceptable and unacceptable paraphrasing.

> "Students are natural economizers. Many students are interested in the shortest route possible through a course. That's why they ask questions such as, 'Will this be on the test?' Copying a paper sometimes looks like a shortcut through an assignment, especially when the student feels overloaded with work already. To combat this cause, assign your paper to be due well before the end-of-term pressures. Remind students that the purpose of the course is to learn and develop skills and not just 'get through.' The more they learn and develop their skills, the more effective they will be in their future lives.
>
> "Students are faced with too many choices, so they put off low priorities. With so many things to do (both of academic and recreational nature), many students put off assignments that do not interest them. A remedy here would be to customize the research topic to include something of real interest to the students or to offer topics with high intrinsic interest to them."

— from Robert Harris at <http://oll.temple.edu/ih/writing/plagiarism_harris.htm>

- "Anti-Plagiarism Strategies for Research Papers," by Robert Harris at <www.virtualsalt.com/antiplag.htm> is a short, well-written guide to this topic. Harris has also written *The Plagiarism Handbook* (Pyrczak Publishing, 2001).

- See also "Plagiarism-proofing Assignments" in this guide.

Benita is rightfully proud of her personal Internet site. She has found pictures, cartoons, and sayings on the Web and copied them to her site. She links to lots of other favorite sites. When asked if her use of items she has found on the Web might violate copyright, she replied that she was careful to use only those things that did not have a copyright notice.

Questions

- What is the property?
- Who is its owner?
- What danger or discomfort might the unethical action cause?
- Is there a parallel in the physical world to this scenario?
- Can you think of other incidents that would fall into this category?

Comments

Myths abound about what is copyrighted on the Internet and what is not. General rule: **Assume everything is copyrighted whether it says so or not.**

Students should also know how to protect their own creative works. Today's "knowledge-based economy" workers (hopefully most) are making a living writing, designing, and inventing new approaches to solving problems. Most of our students of today will become the knowledge workers of tomorrow and will need to know how to protect their creations.

Resources

- Brad Templeton's "10 Big Myths about Copyright Explained" <www.templetons.com/brad/copymyths.html>.

From: School Library Media & Network Communications
Sent: Monday, March 04, 2002 10:45 AM
To: LM_NET@LISTSERV.SYR.EDU
Subject: copyright

The address for the copyright office is <http://www.loc.gov/copyright/>. In essence, anything you create is automatically copyrighted as soon as you create it. To officially copyright a book, or any other written or recorded item, follow the procedures at the above site. The process is to send two copies and some money and LOC will catalog and send you notice of copyright. To acquire a barcode for an item, go to <www.bowker.com>. Barcode numbers are purchased in groups of 10, so often individuals have extras they wouldn't mind sharing or selling to others.

— from George Pilling, Director, District Library Media Services Visalia Learning Center, Visalia Unified School District, 5000 Cypress Ave., Visalia, California 93277. Used with permission.

The Hoax on You

Ever wonder what happened to those odd classmates of yours who got their kicks from pulling fire alarms and making phone calls to strangers asking, "Is your refrigerator running?" Well, my guess is that they are all grown up (sort of) and now spend their time sitting in cubicles creating computer virus hoaxes.

As an unregulated and unedited medium, Internet mail is flooded with hoaxes, urban myths, and chain letters. A great site by the Department of Energy is HoaxBusters at <http://hoaxbusters.ciac.org/> that can help you check these spurious rumors out. Among the most pernicious and frightening hoax e-mails are those that warn users of potentially harmful new viruses.

I'm sure that all of us who have any claim to being techno-savvy have found in our in-box an e-mail that looks like this that was "thoughtfully" forwarded by a colleague, friend, or family member.

> VIRUS WARNING !!!!!!!

> If you receive an e-mail titled "It Takes Guts to Say "Jesus'" DO NOT OPEN
> IT.
> It will erase everything on your hard drive. Forward this letter out to as
> many people as you can. This is a new, very malicious virus and not many
> people know about it. This information was announced yesterday morning from IBM.

There are some immediate clues that a virus warning may be a hoax. According to Joe Wells, Senior Editor of *antivirus online*, a hoax usually has some combination of the following attributes:

- It's a warning message about a virus (or occasionally a Trojan) spreading on the Internet. (Some even describe a "Trojan horse virus." There is no such thing.)

- It's usually from an individual, occasionally from a company, but never from the cited source.

- It warns you not to read or download the supposed virus, and preaches salvation by deletion.

- It describes the virus as having horrific destructive powers and often the ability to send itself by e-mail.

- It usually has lots of words in all caps and loads of exclamation marks.

- It urges you to alert everyone you know, and usually tells you this more than once.

- It seeks credibility by citing some authoritative source as issuing the warning. Usually the source says the virus is "bad" or has them "worried."

- It seeks credibility by describing the virus in specious technical jargon.

Since genuine computer viruses are both common and truly harmful, e-mail users, and especially those of us who teach others about technology, need to be able to determine whether a virus warning is real or a hoax.

Common hoax viruses include the Goodtimes virus, Elf Bowling virus, and the Wobbler virus.

But why make a guess, even if it is an informed one? Since the threat of real damage by a real computer virus is possible, I *always* check out one of the following authoritative sources to see if the suspected hoax virus has been documented:

- Symantec virus hoax page: <www.symantec.com/avcenter/hoax.html>

- McAfee virus hoax page: <http://vil.mcafee.com/hoax.asp>
- Data Fellows hoax warnings: <www.datafellows.com/news/hoax.htm>
- VMyths:

Both the Symantec and McAfee sites are highly credible and contain long lists of known hoax viruses, along with the real ones. I particularly like the Data Fellows page since it has a very good search engine and searches the files of both real and hoax viruses. The VMyth site, while sometimes slow to load, includes tips on dealing with e-mail hoaxes and other supplemental information about them.

Whenever I receive a hoax virus from a concerned colleague or friend, I always alert the one who forwarded the message to the fact that the virus alert was a hoax. I also send them the URLs to these sites so that in the future they can check the authenticity of a virus alert before passing it along.

In the great scheme of things, virus hoaxes tend to be more annoying than dangerous. They do add unwanted traffic to sometimes already overburdened e-mail servers and networks, and they do take time to read, verify, and delete. But probably the real concern we should have about such hoaxes is that they can create complacency about real viruses for some computer users. The boy can only cry "wolf" so many times. Again, real viruses can be damaging and we need to take serious precautions to deal with them.

Finally, be thankful that you didn't get *this* virus!

From: me
Sent: 01 April 2001 09:36
To: EVERYONE!

Subject: FW: ***** VIRUS ALERT *****

If you receive an e-mail entitled 'Badtimes', delete it immediately. Do not open it. Apparently this one is pretty nasty. It will not only erase everything on your hard drive, but it will also delete anything on disks within 20 feet of your computer. It demagnetizes the stripes on ALL of your credit cards. It reprograms your PIN access code, screws up the tracking on your VCR, and uses subspace field harmonics to scratch any CDs you attempt to play.

It will recalibrate your refrigerator's coolness settings so all your ice cream melts and your milk curdles. It will program your phone autodial to call only 1-976 sex line numbers. This virus will mix antifreeze into your fish tank. It will drink all your beer. It will leave dirty socks on the coffee table when you are expecting company.

It will replace your shampoo with engine oil and your engine oil with orange juice, all the while dating your current girl/boyfriend behind your back and billing their hotel rendezvous to your Visa card. It will cause you to run with scissors and throw things in a way that is only fun until someone loses an eye.

It will rewrite your backup files, changing all your active verbs into passive tense and incorporate undetectable misspellings which grossly change the interpretations of key sentences.

If 'Badtimes' is opened in Windows95/98, it will leave the toilet seat up and your hair dryer plugged in dangerously close to a full bath. It will also molecularly rearrange your aftershave/perfume, causing it to smell like dill pickles.

It will install itself into your cistern, block the s-bend and cause your toilet to overflow.

In the worst case scenario, it may stick pins in your eyes.

—Author Unknown

Discussion Questions

1 How does paying for software benefit the user as well as the creator?

2 When does someone "own" an idea? Should the cure for a serious disease be considered property?

3 Can student or employee time be considered property? Can using time at school or work for personal activities be considered property theft?

4 Many warnings about viruses are hoaxes. How can you determine which warnings should be taken seriously and which should be ignored?

5 What new importance does using the Internet for commerce place on consumer education?

6 When should a student report the wrongdoing of another student?

PART FOUR

a(P)propriate Use

This section presents scenarios in which young people must ask: *Does this use of technology have educational value and is it in keeping with the rules of my family, my religion, my school, and my government?*

Appropriate use is often a gray area of technology ethics. Rules made because of scarcity of resources, because of religious values, and for actions that may simply be tasteless or cause discomfort in others are difficult to create and enforce. The range of misuse of technology in this category ranges from the mischievous to the malicious. Place, audience, and purpose can all be factors in whether an action can be gauged as appropriate.

It's sometimes difficult to remember that technology is neutral. It's neither evil nor holy. The same hammer that builds a cathedral can be efficiently used to break the cathedral's windows. The same mechanical engineering that caused the traffic accident takes the injured to the hospital. The same Internet connection that helps students find great information for a term paper can be used to download pornography.

Place

- Most schools allow students to use free time in school to complete personal tasks—to read a book or magazine for enjoyment, to write a letter to a friend, or to draw for pleasure. Technology, too, should be available for students for uses not tied directly to the curriculum—to play games, to send personal e-mail, or to search for Internet information of personal interest. The ethical issue here becomes that of an allocation of resources. For most schools, the demand for technology has outpaced its acquisition. Computers and Internet access are usually in short supply, and priority needs to be given to students who have an academic task to complete.

"This is probably the most complex issue I face in my work. It is so hard dividing what is appropriate usage from inappropriate—we used to want the kids to be learning Internet use and were not so tight-jawed over 'checking soccer scores.' Now I'm not so sure; we spend so much time monitoring and I wonder if our rules would be better enforced if Internet use was research/school use only.

"And the whole word 'appropriate' gets into such cultural/generational connotations—it's prompted some strong discussions in our library. I have found that having as a rule of thumb that if you would be uncomfortable discussing the site with our principal then don't go into it is one the kids understand!"

— from Elizabeth (Libby) Letterly, District Librarian, Williamsville CUSD #15, Williamsville, Illinois. Used with permission.

- Students may use personal technologies inappropriately at school. Personal digital assistants (PDAs), cell phones, pagers, and wireless laptop computers give students the ability to communicate surreptitiously. This form of communication can be used to cheat as well as distract from classroom activities.

Audience

- A good deal of Internet content is tasteless, offensive, and lacking in educational value. Schools should define and teachers should help students understand the qualities and conditions under which an item becomes inappropriate for school use. Students need to understand the concepts of pornography, racism, and sexism. Students may be exposed to information produced by hate groups and political extremists. Such experiences can be springboards to meaningful discussions about propaganda and free speech issues. Materials and topics that students may access from home without parental disapproval are not always appropriate for reading or viewing in schools where a wide range of value systems exist.

- Most schools have harassment policies and appropriate language rules. Students need to understand that harassment is wrong regardless of its medium. And of course, they need to recognize that language used among friends is not always the language used in public discourse of any kind.

Purpose

Technology is neutral. Technology can be used to generate attention and for mischief—two great goals children and young adults have always had.

- Students can use technology to "edit" photographs. Deliberate distortion of events may harm both those involved in the event as well as the reputation of the reporter. While such actions may seem frivolous, journalistic integrity is a serious issue of which even young photographers need to be aware.

- Just as students have created "alternate" school newspapers of a satiric nature, they are now creating "alternate" school Web sites and personal student Web sites that are hosted on non-school computers. Unless the messages on them can be proven to be libelous or threatening, these sites are protected by students' First Amendment rights. School officials need to be careful in how they deal with sites, despite the degree of embarrassment they might cause.

- Disguise, impersonation, and other forms of "trying on" new personalities are common childhood and adolescent behaviors. The anonymity of the Internet allows such impersonation: writing skills and sophistication of thought are the only clues a reader has that a student writer does not have a claimed expertise. Role-playing in a physical context is often seen as both healthy and educational. We need to help students ask when such activities are productive and when they might be harmful.

- Students need to be aware that the Internet is rife with hoaxes and learn to check sites carefully for authenticity and accuracy.

Use these scenarios with your children and students.

Scenario #1

Jack has been using the digital camera to take pictures for the family photo album. Jack has found that he can use a computer program to change the photographs. He has used the program so far to make himself look taller, to blacken out the front tooth of his sister, and to give his dad slightly crossed eyes.

Questions

- What is the inappropriate action?

- Who committed it?

- What danger or discomfort might the unethical action cause?

- Is there a parallel in the physical world to this scenario?

- What new visual literacy skills might critical information seekers need?

- Can you think of other incidents that would fall into this category?

Comments

While this example may seem frivolous or even like "good fun," integrity is a serious issue of which even young writers and photographers need to be aware. Deliberate distortion of events, whether through words or pictures, may harm both those involved in the event as well as the reputation of the reporter. The purpose of a family photo album is to make a record of the activities and appearance of individuals.

Resources

- An interesting discussion of this topic can be found in Bonnie Meltzer's article "Digital Photography—a Question of Ethics." *Learning and Leading with Technology*, December–January, 1995-96 <www.fno.org/may97/digital.html>.

! "As teachers we need to help our students be aware of the issues of imaging. Photo manipulation is not just about using the technology—it is about understanding our society."

—from Bonnie Meltzer

? **Under what circumstances might digital photo editing be appropriate?**

_____

_____

_____

_____

_____

_____

_____

_____

_____

_____

_____

_____

_____

_____

_____

_____

_____

Scenario #2

Just for fun, thirteen-year-old Alice tells the other people on her electronic mailing list that she is twenty years old and a nursing student. Others on the list have begun e-mailing her health-related questions.

Questions

- What is the inappropriate action?

- Who committed it?

- What danger or discomfort might the unethical action cause?

- Is there a parallel in the physical world to this scenario?

- Can you think of other incidents that would fall into this category?

Comments

Disguise, impersonation, and other forms of "trying on" new personalities are common childhood and adolescent behaviors. The anonymity of the Internet limits such impersonation only to the degree that a lack of a young person's writing skills or sophistication of thought allows discovery. Role-playing in a physical context is often seen as both healthy and educational. We need to help our children ask when such activities are productive and when they might be harmful.

Resources

- The Pew Internet & American Life Project "Teenage Life Online" <www.pewinternet.org/reports>.

? How do we know whom to trust in electronic communication formats? In evaluating nonedited sources of information, how important are: accuracy, lack of bias, authority, reliability, currency, and understandability? What other criteria should one use in determining whether to trust information?

Scenario #3

Penelope has found a Web site that has "gross jokes" on it. She prints the pages and shares them with her friends.

Questions

- What is the inappropriate action?

- Who committed it?

- What danger or discomfort might the unethical action cause?

- Is there a parallel in the physical world to this scenario?

- How do you help children know the boundaries of tastelessness? To what extent does such a judgment depend on family values?

- Can you think of other incidents that would fall into this category?

Comments

A good deal of Internet content, if not obscene, is certainly tasteless, offensive, and lacking in educational value. Parents should define and help their children understand the qualities and conditions under which an item becomes inappropriate for use. Children need to understand the concepts of pornography, racism, and sexism.

Children may access information produced by hate groups and political extremists. Such experiences may be springboards to meaningful discussions about propaganda and free speech issues.

Resources

- Read about how one teacher helps students compare Nazi propaganda to current day hate groups in Jeff Carter's June 1998 *Cable in the Classroom* article "High Speed High School."

? **Who determines what is blocked by an Internet filter and what is not in your school? Should parents be able to challenge the availability of Web sites in the same way they can now challenge print materials? To what extent and for what reasons should these things be blocked:**

- games
- chat
- tasteless humor
- racist or sexist materials
- political views on controversial issues
- instructions on creating computer viruses
- sites with dubious health information

_____

_____

_____

_____

_____

_____

_____

_____

_____

_____

_____

_____

_____

The computers in the library always seem to be busy. Otis tells the librarian he is working on a research project, but he actually uses the computer to access the latest soccer scores posted on the Internet.

Questions

- What is the inappropriate action?

- Who committed it?

- What danger or discomfort might the unethical action cause?

- Is there a parallel in the physical world to this scenario?

- Who should be setting the library and technology policies in your school?

- Can you think of other incidents that would fall into this category?

Comments

One of the debates in schools today is whether students should be allowed to use the Internet for personal or recreational purposes. Most of us would agree that priority needs to be given to schoolwork when technological resources are scarce, but computer terminals should never sit empty. And there are some good reasons to allow students personal use of the Internet, especially in the school library:

- **It gives kids a chance to practice skills.** After all, that's why we have "recreational" reading materials in our libraries. Do we really subscribe to *Hot Rod* or *Seventeen* because they're used for research? If we want kids who can do an effective Internet search, read fluently, and love to learn, does it make much difference if they are learning by finding and reading Web pages on the Civil War or playing Civil War games?

- **It gives weight to the penalty of having Internet access taken away.** The penalty for misuse of the Internet is often a suspension of Internet use privileges. As a student, if I were restricted to only schoolwork uses of the Internet and had my Internet rights revoked, I'd pretty much say, "So what?" and wonder what I had to do to get my textbooks taken away as well. But if I am accustomed to using the Internet each morning before school to check on how my favorite sports team was faring, the loss of Internet access as a consequence of misbehavior would be far more serious.

- **It makes the library media center a place kids want to be.** Many of our students love the library for the simple reason that it is often the only place that allows them to read books of personal interest, work on projects that are meaningful, and explore interests that fall outside the curriculum in an atmosphere of relative freedom. Kids need a place like that and we should provide it—even at the Internet terminals.

Resources

- Your library rules and guidelines.

- See "A Good Policy for Policies" in this guide.

Just for fun, Nellie sets the print command on her computer to print 50 copies of an electronic encyclopedia article she's been reading and then walks away.

Questions

- What is the inappropriate action?

- Who committed it?

- What danger or discomfort might the unethical action cause?

- Is there a parallel in the physical world to this scenario?

- Is this an "appropriate use" or "property" issue?

- Can you think of other incidents that would fall into this category?

Comments

Deliberate waste of school materials is not uncommon, and students again need to understand that it is wrong to waste finite resources. As with the vandalism questions, students need to understand that everyone is affected by such activities.

I once had an interesting conversation with a twelve-year-old boy I caught defacing a book in my library. The discussion went like this:

Me: Who owns that book?

Boy: You do. You're the librarian.

Me: Nope. The school owns the book. Who owns the school?

Boy: I don't know.

Me: The taxpayers in the community own the school. Do your parents pay taxes?

Boy: I guess.

Me: Yes, they do. Here's the thing. If you destroy school property, it has to be replaced. That costs money. That may mean higher taxes. If your parents have to spend more of their money on higher taxes, they will have less left over to buy you Christmas presents. It is in *your* best interest that you don't destroy school property.

Resources

- Your school's AUP (Acceptable Use Policy) and building guidelines on technology use. Does it contain a statement about the waste of resources including paper, bandwidth, and file storage space?

Scenario #6

As a joke, Chang sends an e-mail message to his sister who attends a school across town. In this e-mail he uses profanities and racial slurs.

Questions

■ What is the inappropriate action?

■ Who committed it?

■ What danger or discomfort might the unethical action cause?

■ Is this a "technology use" problem or a "harassment" problem?

■ Is there a parallel in the physical world to this scenario?

■ Can you think of other incidents that would fall into this category?

Comments

It was an incident similar to this that helped me understand that I needed to turn to analogous situations in the physical world to help me figure out how to deal with situations in the virtual world. Harassment is harassment, regardless of the medium and the intended target.

Great analogists point out not just the similarities of two things, but their critical differences as well. Are there any critical differences in abusive messages sent via e-mail rather than verbally or by telephone?

Resources

■ Your school's harassment policy.

■ Compare Ethics Questionnaires I and II in the Appendix to this guide. The first contains situations in the virtual world; the second has what may be considered analogous situations in the physical world.

"It is the policy of the school district to maintain a learning and working environment that is free from religious, racial, or sexual harassment and violence. The school district prohibits any form of religious, racial, or sexual harassment and violence.

"It shall be a violation of this policy for any pupil, teacher, administrator, or other school personnel of the school district to harass a pupil, teacher, administrator, or other school personnel through conduct or communication of a sexual nature or regarding religion and race as defined by this policy. (For purposes of this policy, school personnel includes school board members, school employees, agents, volunteers, contractors, or persons subject to the supervision and control of the district.)

"It shall be a violation of this policy for any pupil, teacher, administrator, or other school personnel of the school district to inflict, threaten to inflict, or attempt to inflict religious, racial, or sexual violence upon any pupil, teacher, administrator, or other school personnel.

"The school district will act to investigate all complaints, either formal or informal, verbal or written, of religious, racial, or sexual harassment or violence, and to discipline or take appropriate action against any pupil, teacher, administrator, or other school personnel who is found to have violated this policy."

— from the Mankato Public Schools (Minnesota) Harassment and Violence Board Policy

Clark downloads a page with sexually explicit photographs from the Internet to a computer in the classroom. He shows its contents to others in his class.

Questions

■ What is the inappropriate action?

■ Who committed it?

■ What danger or discomfort might the unethical action cause?

■ Is there a parallel in the physical world to this scenario?

■ If an inappropriate site is reached accidentally, how can one develop the trust needed for a student to report the error to a parent or school staff person?

■ Can you think of other incidents that would fall into this category?

Comments

Kids are kids. Curious and ornery. Some seek attention from outlandish behaviors. Technology gives children one more opportunity for such behavior.

In my experience adults tend to overreact to incidents of technology abuse since they simply can't relate to them. The opportunities such as Clark has above simply were not there when most of us were kids.

Should Clark have brought in a *Playboy* magazine, I doubt the school would prohibit him from reading (or looking at pictures) for the rest of the year. Should the school prohibit Clark from using the Internet after an incident like the one described above?

Resources

■ See "Mischief and Mayhem" at the end of Part Four.

■ See box on page 71 for some guidelines in creating fair consequences for Internet misuse.

? **How should you as a parent or teacher respond (and want your children to respond) if an offensive web site is accessed accidentally?**

_____

_____

_____

_____

_____

_____

_____

_____

_____

_____

_____

_____

_____

_____

_____

Linda suffers from an eating disorder. She has been accessing "pro-anorexia" sites on the Internet and participating in chats with other young people who share her condition in order to get support for the continuation of her behaviors.

Questions

- What is the inappropriate action?

- Who committed it?

- What danger or discomfort might the unethical action cause?

- Is there a parallel in the physical world to this scenario?

- Can you think of other incidents that would fall into this category?

Comments

Search long and hard enough, almost any point of view or opinion can be found somewhere on the Net. Our roles as teachers, librarians, and parents have in significant ways changed from dispensing information to helping young people critically evaluate information. Old people still have a role to play in the educational world.

Resources

- Kathy Schrock's Web pages that address the critical evaluation of Web sites at <http://school.discovery.com/schrockguide/eval.html> are among the best on the Web. These come in a range of reading levels to be used with all ages of students.

"
"Developing an eating disorder is no easy task. Becoming an anorexic, for example, requires months, even years, of obsessive, destructive tunnel vision. Anorexia demands absolute, single-minded dedication. It's exhausting—and it can be extraordinarily lonely.

"That's where technology comes in. Thanks to the wonders of the Internet, anorexics and would-be anorexics around the globe can access more than 400 Web sites designed solely for them. Need to know how to disguise your weight loss so concerned (read: jealous) friends will stop hounding you to eat? Looking for a few words of support as you launch into your latest deprivation diet? Or perhaps you'd like to know the tricks for satisfying that pesky weekly weigh-in at the doctor's office? It's all right here."

— from Time.com < www.time.com/>, Tuesday, July 31, 2001

All the students at Peter and Paul's school have been given PDAs (personal digital assistants—small, handheld computers). The boys have been using the wireless transmission features to exchange notes and test answers in class.

Questions

- What is the inappropriate action?

- Who committed it?

- What danger or discomfort might the unethical action cause?

- Is there a parallel in the physical world to this scenario?

- How does a school prevent nearly undetectable forms of cheating?

- Can you think of other incidents that would fall into this category?

Comments

While much effort has gone into preventing plagiarism in schools, other forms of cheating are also made possible by technology. If a product can be used, it can be abused.

Cheating needs to be defined by the school and school-wide uniform policies developed and enforced to prevent it.

Resources

- Check the Appendix "Cheating and How to Avoid It" in this book.

> **COMMUNICATIONS-RELATED HEADLINES** for January 31, 2002
> PUPILS AND PORN AND GAMES, OH MY
> Issue: *Edtech*
>
> "Virginia's Henrico County Public Schools distributed over 11,000 Apple iBooks to its high school students, some of whom promptly began downloading pornography, playing games in class, and trading music and movie files. 'We started out giving them total freedom,' said Charles Stallard, the Henrico district's director of technology. But now, new rules attempt to 'cut out the extraneous activity unrelated to the instructional program.' Students only have filtered access to the Web and Instant Messaging is locked out of the school environment. The difficulties in Henrico County illustrate the many issues that districts have to consider when implementing a one-to-one computing program. Technology is only one part. 'All too often we put this issue in much too narrow of a frame,' said Keith Krueger, executive director of the Consortium for School Networking. 'Information literacy is a much larger issue. We have to make sure kids become their own filter.' That means teaching students about copyright issues, teaching them to evaluate information and realizing that not everything on the Net is accurate."
>
> — from *Wired*, by Katie Dean <http://www.wired.com/news/school/0,1383,50001,00.html>

Bill has created an "alternative" school Web site on a commercial server. His site satirizes school activities, holds doctored photos of staff members, and makes fun of fellow students. When the principal discovers the Web site, he withdraws the recommendation he has written for a college scholarship for which Bill has applied.

Questions

- What is the inappropriate action?

- Who committed it?

- What danger or discomfort might the unethical action cause?

- Is there a parallel in the physical world to this scenario?

- Can you think of other incidents that would fall into this category?

Comments

Students are also protected by the First Amendment. Unless libel or terrorist threats are made on a student Web page, school officials need to respect the rights of students.

Resources

- The American Civil Liberties Union Web site at <www.aclu.org/> lists a number of current student free speech issues, a number dealing with technology-based communication. From the home page click on the "Free Speech" link on the right side of the page and on the Free Speech page, click on the link to "Students."

SAN FRANCISCO, CA—In a case with important implications for free speech on the Internet, the American Civil Liberties Union of Northern California has asked a Superior Court to dismiss a lawsuit aimed at shutting down a Web site that provides student reviews of the teachers at San Francisco City College.

The lawsuit was filed in San Francisco Superior Court City College by professor Daniel Curzon Brown, who objects to what students had to say about his teaching.

The ACLU, on behalf of Ryan Lathouwers, the creator of the Teacher Review Web site, says that the speech is protected under the First Amendment. Other defendants in the suit, the San Francisco Community College District, which is the governing body of City College, and the Associated Students of City College, agree.

"The Teacher Review Web site is a perfect example of how the Internet functions as a unique and valuable information source," said ACLU of Northern California staff attorney Ann Brick. "If permitted to proceed, this case would sound the death knell for any Web site or bulletin board allowing members of the public to exchange opinions."

ACLU Press Release: 01-31-00

Debbie is running for class president. She uses an electronic mailing list (listserv) to send regular e-mails to all the students in her class explaining her platform and actions she would take as president.

Questions

- What is the inappropriate action?

- Who committed it?

- What danger or discomfort might the unethical action cause?

- Is there a parallel in the physical world to this scenario?

- Can you think of other incidents that would fall into this category?

Comments

Most Acceptable Use Policies state that the school's resources should not be used for personal gain. Does running for student office constitute personal gain? Does selling candy for DECA? Does hosting a Boy Scout Web page? Does running a listserv for a state professional organization?

The question becomes: should we take a hard line approach to enforcing a school AUP? No e-mail for non-school purposes. No recreational or personal use of the Internet. No creative or experimental uses of the technologies. Stringent application of all guidelines. High levels of monitoring. Maximum filter settings (Starting to sound like a nice place to go to school or work?)

I tend to interpret the policy rather liberally. It has everything to do with school climate. I can't help but think that the personal use of the Internet affects one's performance as a student or teacher. It makes the school a more comfortable place to be.

Teachers and kids have enough stress in their lives. If a joke in a personal e-mail lessens the stress and makes for happier residents, this is a good thing.

I would strongly advise that a school committee, rather than a single technology director, administrator, or technician, should make the policies and rules that affect school climate. See the comments under "A Good Policy for Policies" in this book for more details.

Resources

- Your school's student handbook.

- Your school's technology committee.

- Your school's rules on related practices: bulletin boards, PA systems, recreational library use, etc.

Alex is observed by the library media specialist accessing "adult" sites. When asked about his choice of sites, he readily admits that he has chosen to do his senior thesis on Internet pornography.

Questions

- What is the inappropriate action?

- Who committed it?

- What danger or discomfort might the unethical action cause?

- Is there a parallel in the physical world to this scenario?

- Can you think of other incidents that would fall into this category?

Comments

In her book *Computer Ethics, Etiquette and Safety for the 21st-Century Student*, Nancy Willard suggests Eight Ethical Decision-Making Strategies. The "Trusted Adult Test" is one which all students need to ask, "What would your mom or dad, guardian or other adult who is important in your life think (about your action)?"

I can't help but believe most human beings are basically good—even adolescents—and they care about what we as adults think of them. Let's let them make decisions, let them make mistakes, let them learn. It's our role as teachers and parents.

Resources

- "Teacher's Introduction" in *Computer Ethics, Etiquette and Safety for the 21st-Century Student* by Nancy Willard (ISTE, 2002).

? One little explored area of teaching values concerns how to interpret information that may have a political bias. A teacher or librarian may rank the trustworthiness of the sources below as they appear in this list from high to low. A parent may rank them from low to high. How do we (or should we) help students filter politics out of their information reliability assessment?

- Center for Disease Control
- Newsweek
- A nonfiction bestseller
- Insurance companies/HMOs
- Personal Web pages/chatrooms
- Radio talk shows

_____

_____

_____

_____

_____

_____

_____

_____

_____

_____

_____

_____

_____

_____

_____

See Lawrence Magid's thoughtful article "Filtering Programs Useful But Far From Perfect" at <www.safekids.com/articles/filtering2000.htm>.

Facts about Filters

A filter is a software program that attempts to block access to parts of the Internet deemed unsafe or inappropriate for some users. Sexual content, controversial political beliefs, and instructions on making harmful devices such as bombs are often targeted as areas for filtering. Some filters can block file types or entire Internet protocols such as e-mail or chatrooms.

Schools that wish to receive federal E-Rate funds are mandated to have filters or other technological measures in place that are meant to block access to sites deemed "harmful to minors."

Even if a filter is in place, some important considerations still need to be made:

- Filters are *never* 100% reliable.

- "Cheats" for many filters are readily available to users who wish to get around them.

- Filters need to be continuously updated, often at additional expense.

- Filters often block sites that *are* appropriate for children.

- Filtering manufacturers may have a political agenda—blocking sites because of a political point of view.

- Filters shift responsibility for appropriate use from the user to the installer of the program.

- Parents may need their child's help installing the filter. :-)

A study conducted in 2002 by the Electronic Freedom Foundation on Internet filtering devices at <www.eff.org/Censorship/Academic_edu/Censorware/net_block_report/20020918_eff_pr.html> reveals some interesting numbers:

- Schools that implement Internet blocking software with the least restrictive settings will block between 1/2% and 5% of search results based on state-mandated curriculum topics.

- Schools that implement Internet blocking software with the most restrictive settings will block up to 70% of search results based on state-mandated curriculum topics.

Internet filters obviously have a wide range of restrictiveness. Depending on the product, the product's settings, and the ability to override the filter to permit access to individual sites, filters can either block a high percentage of the Internet resources (specific Web sites, e-mail, chatrooms, etc.) or a relatively small number of sites.

If a school is to give students and staff as much intellectual freedom as possible, it needs to:

- Base its choice of filters not on cost or convenience, but on features and customizability.

- Use the least restrictive settings of installed filters.

- Generously use the override lists in its Internet filters.

- Configure at least one machine that is completely unblocked in each library media center so that questionably blocked sites can be reviewed and immediately accessed by staff and students if found to be useful.

- Continue to help develop and teach the values students need to be self-regulating Internet users.

- Continue to educate and inform parents and the public about school Internet uses and issues.

- Continue to create learning environments that promote the use of the Internet for positive purposes.

Mischief and Mayhem

Ex abusu non arguitur in usum. (The abuse of a thing is no argument against its use.)

A very distraught high school teacher came to see me last week. It seems an anonymous someone had sent an e-mail message using Aaron's return address. The message wasn't very nice at all, and Aaron was insistent that the technology department (meaning me) find a way of keeping this from ever happening again. "A career could be ruined by such an incident," he fumed.

While I could certainly understand why he was upset, I don't believe I gave Aaron the answer he was looking for. No foolproof mechanical means of keeping people from sending e-mail under a borrowed or assumed name (spoofing) exists. Any e-mailer or Web browser allows a user to change the return address. Anonymous mail services are easy to find. Digital signatures are still on the horizon.

Network management systems let us keep track of who was using what computer to do what when. But when an incident of suspected misuse occurs, who has the time to check the logs of every networked computer in the building? We can't even assume that the e-mail was sent from the school. It is as (or more) likely that the offending e-mail in Aaron's name was sent from a private home, the local university, or the techno-coffee shop a few blocks away. Should we even automatically assume it was a student?

Sending an anonymous or misattributed e-mail is analogous to an obscene phone call or an unsigned note. Easier to do perhaps because there are no fingerprints, no voice, and no handwriting left in the ether. But trying to remember that similar things happened before there were computers and networks is sometimes hard to do. Electronic communication is still largely strange to most of us, and human beings tend to be wary of that which is strange.

Aaron is a good teacher. He's young, enthusiastic, and likes to use technology with his kids. His character and reputation will keep him from being seriously considered as the sender of the bad e-mail. My sense is that we may all have this happen to us sooner or later. We can only hope our own reputations carry us as well.

Misuse of technology is not uncommon in schools. No matter how diligent teachers and administrators try to be, students will work around the new password, print 500 copies of Miss April to the office computer, wantonly trash files, or engage in electronic harassment. It is the today's version of tipping outhouses, stealing watermelons, or putting the Volkswagen on the school roof. The problem is that we adults can't identify with the electronic havoc from which our students now seem to get so much delight, since we ourselves have not committed it and most likely don't understand how to do it.

It starts young too. Our middle school was having a bad time with its ceiling mounted televisions randomly turning on and off, switching channels, and gaining and losing volume. The sets worked in the shop, but back in the school building they acted up again. Until one day a teacher discovered a student with a special watch. It had a built in television remote. What a delightful sense of power that student must have felt for a few weeks!

Of course not all technology misuse is harmless. Electronic threats to the President have resulted in visits by the Secret Service to a number of schools. The potential for destroyed data is very real, as "crackers" gain a Robin Hood-like status with some students. An obscene message, regardless of its method of delivery, can be traumatizing, and the thought of a computer that controls a dam's flood gates being unofficially accessed is terrifying. Intentional or unintentional, the potential harm resulting in technological mayhem is quite real.

How can we as educators respond?

- If a student's use of technology violates a school rule, deal with it as you would any incident. The consequence of sending a harassing e-mail should be the same as the consequence of sending a harassing paper note. Searching a disk should be treated no differently than searching a locker.

- Set up as few "challenges" to students who delight in getting around the system as possible. If a machine does not need a password, don't give it one. Rely on human control and observation rather than mechanical controls.

- Teach netiquette at the same time you teach technology skills. Allow student input into technology policy making and planning.

- Give students ownership of the system. One of our technicians deliberately seeks out the school's potential crackers and gives them responsibility for lab security. What's the expression— "It takes a thief...?"

- Don't take an incident any more seriously than it really is. If we are truly giving students choices, we have to accept the fact that some students are going to make bad ones. But learning and growth result.

It is human nature to test a system, cause mischief, and subvert authority. But humans also live by rules, act for the common good, and respect the rights of others. Good cybercitizens can be developed if we as adults don't blindly overreact.

Discussion Questions

1 Can some actions be considered inappropriate for some young people and not others depending on their family beliefs? Can some actions be considered inappropriate based on the age of the individual? How does the concept of "in loco parentis" apply in the digital world?

2 Can the personal use of a technology resource owned by a school or business ever be appropriate? Under what circumstances?

3 Should a student be allowed to use the school networks and e-mail to run for a school office?

4 What is the definition of "pornographic?" How would you define "hate group?" Are there ever times when a pornographic or hate group site could be viewed as appropriate?

5 How does electronic vandalism or waste of public property harm the individual citizen?

6 Should schools and homes install Internet filters?

PART FIVE

Teaching and Promoting Ethical Behaviors

What Children and Young Adults Need to Understand

As should be pretty obvious by now, our children are growing up in a world that has been made far more complex because it is virtual as well as physical. While in many cases the ethical decisions that need to be made seem relatively black and white, there are many cases to which careful thought must be given and for which there are no absolutes.

It is also obvious that our children need to understand and apply home and school rules as well as local and national laws that apply to information technology use, especially those related to privacy, property, and appropriateness as described in the last three sections. Young people need to know the consequences, both immediate and long term, for themselves and for society if they choose to act against those rules and laws.

As students, as employees, and as citizens, people of all ages need to know that the ability of officials to catch individuals breaking these rules and codes of conduct is growing. Network security systems are becoming more sophisticated in tracking who uses what resource at what time. Young people need to realize that most Web browsers keep a viewable log of recently visited sites, that most e-mail includes a return address, and that some schools and homes are using programs that record all the keystrokes made during a computer session. Our children need to understand that organizations have the right to search file server space and read the e-mail of students (and staff), especially if there is probable cause for a search. Electronic fingerprints, virtual footprints, and broken digital locks are growing more visible each day.

Proactive teachers like Ann Brachwitz from the Germantown (Pennsylvania) Friends School design activities that simulate choices students need to make and stimulate class discussions.

Ann has developed four specific lessons:

- Peeking and Privacy
- Creativity and Copyrights
- E-mail Mania
- Wild Wild Web

See Joyce Valenza's "Teaching Ethics in a World of Electronics" for more information <http://joycevalenza.com/ethics.html>.

Children need to understand both their rights and responsibilities related to information technology use. In your home and your child's school, is Internet access a right or a privilege? As the Internet becomes a more indispensable source of information and learning activities, it may become viewed as an integral part of one's right to an education. We have an obligation to teach our young people that they have a right to due process if charged with a violation of rules or laws. Our children's schools' Acceptable Use Policies need to articulate what that due process entails. And pragmatically, our children need to know how to protect themselves and their data from strangers, hackers, computer viruses, and unauthorized use.

"Schools are starting to realize that, as computer use becomes a part of daily life even for kindergartners, part of their job is to teach not just technical skills but also the ethics that go along with living in a wired world. In Texas, the 'essential knowledge and skills inventory' stipulates that all third grade students must know how to e-mail and that all sixth grade students know how to create a database.

"Penni Jones, the Allen (Texas) Independent School District's technology coordinator, has incorporated an innovative program called 'Chip and Friends' into the schools in her district. Begun in 1992 as an outreach program of the Lawrence Livermore National Laboratory, the curriculum was spun off into an hour-long videotape that uses puppets and a squishy computer named Chip to teach little kids right and wrong online. It is available through the Computer Learning Foundation in Palo Alto, California."

— from Elizabeth Weise, "Cracking the hacker myth," *USA Today*, May 6, 1998

What Activities Teach Ethical Behaviors?

Business Ethics magazine suggests that businesses take a proactive approach to ethical issues. That advice is also good for homes, libraries, and classrooms. As adults, we must:

- *Articulate our personal values.* Talk to your children about what you believe to be ethical conduct online. Set clear limits about what is allowed and what is not allowed. Be knowledgeable about your child's school's Acceptable Use Policy. See if the labs, libraries, and classrooms your children use display lists and create handouts of conduct codes.

- *Reinforce ethical behaviors and react to non-ethical behaviors.* Technology use behaviors should be treated no differently than other behaviors—good or bad—and the consequences of such behaviors should be the same. It is important not to overreact to incidences of technological misuse, either. If you caught your child reading *Playboy* would you take away all his or her reading privileges?

- *Model ethical behaviors.* All of us learn more from what others do than what they say. The ethical conduct we expect from our children, we ourselves must display. Verbalization of how we personally make decisions is a very powerful teaching tool. It's useless to lecture about intellectual property when we as adults use pirated software!

- *Create environments that help children avoid temptations.* Computer screens that are easily monitored (no pun intended), passwords not written down or left easily found, and getting into the habit of logging out of secure network systems all help remove the opportunities for technology misuse. I strongly recommend that home computers that can connect to the Internet only be placed in living rooms, family rooms, kitchens or dens—*not* in a child's bedroom. The presence of an adult is a far more effective means of assuring good behavior than any filtering software.

- *Encourage discussion of ethical issues.* "Cases," whether from news sources or from actual events from your child's experience, can provide superb discussion starters and should be used when young people are actually learning computer skills. Children need practice in creating meaningful analogies between the virtual world and the physical world. How is reading other people's e-mail without their permission like and unlike reading their physical mail?

- *Stress the consideration of principles rather than relying on a detailed set of rules.* Although sometimes more difficult to enforce in a consistent manner, a set of a few guidelines rather than lengthy set of specific rules is more beneficial to children in the long run. By applying guidelines rather than following rules, young learners engage in higher level thinking processes and internalize behaviors that will continue into their adult lives. Think how wonderfully the Golden Rule applies to so many situations: Treat others as you yourself would like to be treated. Children who have internalized that concept can make good ethical choices whether in the classroom, on the playground, or at the supper table.

- *Help children understand that ethical behaviors are in their own long-term best interest.* Rules of society exist because they tend to make the world a safer, more secure, and more opportunity-filled place.

Additionally, children's understandings of ethic concepts need to be assessed. Technology use privileges should not be given until an individual has demonstrated that he or she knows and can apply ethical standards and school policies. While this is done informally at home, schools need to test appropriate use prior to students gaining online privileges such as e-mail accounts or Internet access. Teachers or librarians should keep evidence of testing on file in case there is a question of whether there has been instruction on appropriate use.

Schools also have an obligation to educate their parents about ethical technology use. Through school newsletters, talks at parent organization meetings, and through school orientation programs, the school staff needs to inform and enlist the aid of parents in teaching and enforcing good technology practices.

Finally, ethical instruction needs to be ongoing. A single lesson, a single incident, or a single curriculum strand will not suffice. All of us—parents, teachers, librarians, and community members—must integrate ethical instruction into every activity that uses technology. Good parenting and teaching is an ongoing process even, or perhaps especially, in the virtual world.

Policies, Guidelines and Rules Schools Need to Have

School officials who understand the ethical issues surrounding technology use can use those understandings to formulate policies, rules, and guidelines for its use by both students and staff. These rules should be in written form, readily available, and frequently revised.

Acceptable Use Policies

Most schools now have adopted an "Acceptable Use Policy" that governs the use of the Internet and other information technologies and networks in a school. This policy needs to be school board adopted and should apply to both staff and student technology use. Everyone in the school, as well as parents, needs to know and understand these policies. The Mankato Schools' Acceptable Use Policy, for example, describes the role of networked technologies in education, the due processes by which violators of the policy are protected, and some explicit rules of use.

Web Site Guidelines

Schools that have created Web sites will need to establish guidelines. These guidelines usually address:

- the purpose of the Web site

- the identification and responsibility for oversight of the Web site

- the persons authorized to create and maintain pages on the site

- content standards for the site including subject matter and quality

- privacy safeguards for students placing work on the site including guidelines for photographs, e-mail addresses, and whether parental permission needs to be given

- copyright guidelines for student work

- a short restatement of general technology use policies of the district that apply to the use of the Web site specifically

- technical standards including using standard HTML conventions, limiting the size and amount of graphic files, establishing the date and authorship of pages, and establishing a schedule for page updating and revisions

- contact information for questions or problems about the site

Building and Library Rules

Individual buildings and library media centers may choose to create rules for technology use that are more specific to their own programs. These rules, which are often driven by the availability of technology, should be created by a building-wide committee rather than a single individual. Such rules might cover:

- the appropriate use of e-mail, chatrooms, and recreational use of the Internet

- the downloading and use of bandwidth intensive files such as those that carry sound and video

- printing policies

- length of time an individual student may use an Internetworked computer

- use of privately owned and downloaded software (software installation policy) by both students and staff

- where and how student-created files are stored

- if and how student and staff activities are monitored while using technology

Deborah Maehs, LMS, from Kingfisher Middle School, Kingfisher, Oklahoma, offers this plagiarism-prevention plan in workshops for her staff and fellow professionals:

I. Lay the foundation

- Read *Student Cheating and Plagiarism in the Internet Era* by Lothrop and Foss

- Establish a building honor code

- Establish a standardized policy on plagiarism among faculty

- Address plagiarism in assessment rubrics

- Be familiar with online sources for research papers

II. Examine the writing purpose—ask "Why are we doing this?"

III. Teach the writing process

Plagiarism Guidelines

Increasingly, buildings are writing specific guidelines that address plagiarism. These guidelines clearly state in language appropriate to the age level of the student:

- what plagiarism is

- how to correctly identify sources, including text and graphics from both print and electronic sources, interviews, and ideas from a variety of sources including conversations, songs, television programs, computer programs, etc.

- the ideas that do not need to be documented, including personal experience, generally accepted facts, and results from personally-conducted experiments

- the penalties for submitting work that has been plagiarized

- a warning of how plagiarism can be detected

    Some schools have chosen to incorporate plagiarism guidelines into general "cheating" guidelines.

Looking for sources of classroom activities that help teach technology ethics? Try:

"Strategies for Teaching Children Responsible Use of Technology" from *Computer Learning Month* <www. computerlearning.org/articles/EthicTch.htm>.

Nancy Willard's book *Computer Ethics, Etiquette & Safety for the 21st-Century Student* (ISTE, 2002)

What Schools Need to Do to Teach and Encourage Ethical Behaviors

Schools must take a proactive approach to creating ethical technology users. Informing students and staff about ethical issues, discussing technology uses in light of ethical values, detecting technology misuse, and enforcing the appropriate use of technology resources are ongoing tasks. No single approach to educating students about the proper use of technology can be relied on to create ethical users of information technologies.

1 **Staff development activities need to address ethical issues and develop an awareness and understanding of these issues in all adults who work with students.** These activities can be specific inservices or integrated into general teacher technology classes. Library and technology departments can raise the awareness of ethical issues by sending short e-mail "bulletins" to district staff listservs.

2 **Policies, guidelines, and rules need to be readily available to staff, students, and parents.** Basic rules for technology use should be available as handouts in offices, media centers, and classrooms. They should be posted to the school's Web site. Many schools print them in staff and student handbooks. Each year technology rules should be explained and discussed during student orientation to the school and to the media center, during new staff orientation, in classes at the beginning of major research projects, and during parent open houses.

3 **All staff members should be encouraged to articulate personal values in situations where ethical decisions must be made and should encourage the discussion of ethical issues as a part of classroom instruction.** "Cases," whether from news sources or from actual school events, can provide superb discussion starters and should be used when students are actually learning computer skills. Students need practice in creating meaningful analogies between the virtual world and the physical world. Frances Jacobson Harris from the University Laboratory High School Library in Urbana, Illinois, uses an electronic bulletin board to present ethical issues and to display student reactions.

4 **All staff members should model ethical behaviors of technology use.** Students learn more from what we do than what we say. Verbalization of how we personally make decisions is a very powerful teaching tool.

5 **All staff members should reinforce ethical behaviors and react to non-ethical behaviors.** Technology use behaviors should be treated no differently than other behaviors—good or bad—and the consequences of student behaviors should be the same. It is important not to overreact to incidences of technology misuse. Should a student bring inappropriate reading material to school, we do not ban reading for that child. Should a student access inappropriate material on the Internet, we should not ban the child's use of the Internet.

6 Students' understandings of ethical concepts need to be assessed.

Technology use privileges should not be given to students until they have demonstrated that they know and can apply ethical standards and school policies. Testing of appropriate use needs to be done prior to students gaining online privileges such as e-mail accounts or Internet access. The teacher should keep evidence of testing on file in case there is a question of whether there has been instruction on appropriate use.

7 Schools must work to create environments that help students avoid the temptation to misuse technology resources.

Computer screens that are easily monitored, passwords not written down or easily guessed, and the habit of logging out of secure network systems all help remove the opportunities for technology misuse in a classroom. Schools that remotely monitor student computer use with special software should alert students of this ability. Students should not be left unattended where computer access is possible. Curricular purposes for technology use should be stressed.

?

To: dougj@doug-johnson.com
Subject: acceptable use policy violations

I am a school library media specialist at a public school. While my school has an acceptable use policy, we do not have a list of appropriate consequences for violations. All students get the same consequence of one month of no Internet use regardless of the infraction. Do you have a list of logical consequences for the various types on violations or do you know where I could get such a thing? Thanks for your time and help.

Sincerely,
Maureen

Hi Maureen,

Each of our buildings has its own set of consequences that are set by the librarian and library committee. I might suggest some guidelines that could be used in formulating such a policy:

1 Look at the consequence for other improper activities that already exist in your school. If a student sends a harassing e-mail, for example, follow your regular policy on harassment.

2 Graduate the penalties. I would not deny students access to the Internet for an extended period of time for a first infraction of the rules. (You would not ban a child from reading if he or she was caught reading something inappropriate.) If the inappropriate behavior repeats itself, increase the penalties.

3 Bring parents in on any ethical use violation.

4 If you do not already do so, allow students personal use the Internet. If the Internet-networked computers are not being used for curricular purposes, students should be allowed to research topics of personal interest (that are not dangerous or pornographic, of course), send e-mail to friends, etc. One reason for allowing this is that students are far less likely to risk loss of Internet privileges if that means losing access to things that they enjoy.

5 Make sure your rules are clearly stated, available, and consistently enforced.

Hope this helps. All the best,

Doug

What might a set of home Internet rules include?

Dad's Household Computer Rules

- Do not break the law. I don't have money for bail or fines.

- Do not invade others' privacy (and I will respect yours).

- Do not give out *any* personal information about yourself or the family.

- Be truthful about who you say you are in online communications.

- Talk to me if anything about a Web site concerns or confuses you. I know that bad sites can be accessed accidentally.

- Don't download and install software without permission. I mean it.

- Be as smart, skeptical, and cautious online as you are elsewhere.

- Don't do anything you wouldn't do if I were watching you. I just might be.

8 **Teachers and media specialists must begin to prevent plagiarism by designing good research projects.** A great deal of effort goes into detecting plagiarism, but not much thought goes into preventing it. Well-designed assignments that are personal, ask for higher level thinking, and require creative solutions to problems or answers to questions significantly decrease the ability and temptation to plagiarize the materials of others.

9 **Schools should use standards that stress ethical use of information and technology.** Both the International Society for Technology in Education and American Association of School Librarians' student standards for technology and information literacy have ethical use components. These should be used as guides when writing local curricula.

10 **Schools have an obligation to educate parents about ethical technology use.** Through school newsletters, talks at parent organization meetings, and through school orientation programs, the school staff needs to inform and enlist the aid of parents in teaching and enforcing good technology practices. Parents should be made aware of the American Association of School Librarians online course, which has been written just for them.

11 **Ethical instruction needs to be ongoing.** A single lesson, a single unit, or a single curriculum strand will not suffice. All teachers, librarians, and staff members must integrate ethical instruction into every activity that uses technology.

What Homes Need to Do to Teach and Encourage Ethical Behaviors

1 **Parents need to become educated about the ethical and safety issues regarding technology use.** By reading guides, related newspaper and magazine articles, and attending information sessions offered by schools and community organizations, parents can stay informed about the problems and dangers associated with technology use—especially online computer use.

2 **Rules for computer and other technology use need to be clearly stated.** Basic rules for technology use should be short, simple, and clear. By posting a list of rules by the home computer, parents can help children remember them.

3 **Parents should articulate personal values in situations where ethical decisions must be made and encourage the discussion of ethical issues as a part of family discussions**. "Cases," whether from news sources or from actual school events, can provide superb discussion starters and should be used when students are actually learning computer skills.

4 **Parents should model ethical behaviors of technology use.** Children learn more from what we do than from what we say. Verbalization of how we personally make decisions is a very powerful teaching tool.

5 **Parents should reinforce ethical behaviors and react to non-ethical behaviors.** Technology use behaviors should be treated no differently than other behaviors—good or bad—and the consequences of children's behaviors should be the same. It is important not to overreact to incidences of technology misuse. Building a trusting relationship between parent and child is of tremendous importance.

6 **Parents should work to create environments that help students avoid the temptation to misuse technology resources.** Computers that are connected to the Internet should be in common family areas—the kitchen, family room, den, or living room—*not* in a child's bedroom.

7 **Ethical instruction needs to be ongoing.** Each skill taught or resource provided by parent for a child needs a discussion on its ethical use.

What Our State and National Professional Associations Need to Do to Teach and Encourage Ethical Behaviors

1 **Recognize that ethical technology use by students** should be a part of all technology standards and competencies imbedded in curricula written by the organization.

2 **Revise professional standards** to specifically include ethical technology use by membership.

3 **Develop training materials and learning opportunities for members** as a part of the formal continuing education efforts of the organization.

4 **Encourage sharing of effective materials** about and an in-depth discussion of technology ethics issues by the organization's membership.

5 **Make technology ethics a part of pre-professional training programs and articulate specific competencies.** Make ethical technology use an area studied in accreditation visits.

6 **Encourage representatives of the organization or profession to speak clearly** and knowledgeably about technology ethics issues as related to the field.

A Fence or an Ambulance
Joseph Malins—1895

'Twas a dangerous cliff, and it fair scared folks stiff,
But the view from the top was so pleasant,
That they swallowed their fear, and there crashed down
   each year
Full many a squire and peasant.

"Something's got to be done," said the people as one,
But answers did not at all tally.
Some said, "Put a fence 'round the edge of the cliff."
Some, "An ambulance down in the valley!"

Debate raged and stormed, and a Study was formed,
And they might have been arguing yet,
But a solution was found: "Let's pass the hat 'round,
And see how much money we get."

A collection was made to accumulate aid,
And dwellers in byway and alley
Gave pounds, shillings and pence—not to furnish a fence
But an ambulance down in the valley.

"For the cliff is all right if you're careful," they said;
"And if folks ever slip and are dropping,
It isn't the slipping that hurts them so much
As the shock down below—when they're stopping."

So for years (you'll have heard) as these mishaps occurred
Quick forth would the rescuers sally,
To pick up the victims who fell from the cliff,
With the ambulance down in the valley.

Then an old sage remarked: "It's a marvel to me
That people give far more attention
To repairing results than to stopping the cause,
When they'd much better aim at prevention.

"Let us stop at its source all this mischief," cried he,
"Come, neighbors and friends let us rally,
If the cliff we will fence we might almost dispense
With the ambulance down in the valley."

"He is wrong in his head," the majority said;
"He would end all our earnest endeavor.
He's a man who would shirk this responsible work
But we will support it forever.

"Aren't we picking up all, just as fast as they fall,
In giving them care we don't dally?
It's plain that a fence is of no consequence,
If the ambulance works in the valley."

Plagiarism-proofing Assignments

When I hear the stories of rampant plagiarism being discussed in the media or on the Net, an old poem comes to mind. "A Fence or an Ambulance" by Joseph Malins argues that it is better to spend one's efforts on preventing an unwise action (building a fence on the top of the cliff) than cleaning up afterwards (providing an ambulance at the bottom of it).

I believe too much effort is expended in education trying to "catch" plagiarism in student work. Teachers and media specialists are using various Web services and techniques using search engines to determine if or how much of student writing is lifted from online sources.

Our time as parents and educators is better spent in creating assignments, especially those that involve research, that minimize the likelihood of plagiarism in the first place. Rather than making assignments that can be easily plagiarized and then contriving methods for detecting or reducing copying, why not do a little work upfront to design projects that require original, thoughtful research?

Consider the scenarios on the next page.

Scenario #1

Mike is a wonderful young man. Handsome, intelligent, caring, and sweet, he's better than about 99% of the rest of the kids out there. But the one thing he is not is much of a scholar. He is diligent, but perfunctory, about his school assignments.

On occasion, however, Mike gets very excited about his schoolwork. Science fair is one of those times. He spends weekends conducting experiments, visiting the library, searching Web sites, making graphs, taking photos, and carefully designing a presentation board illustrating his findings. He is involved, working entire days consumed by his task.

One of his best projects was one he completed in the fifth grade. He wanted to determine what substance, when applied to ice, would melt it the most quickly. He drilled holes in the bottoms of four or five aluminum pie plates, taped over the holes, and then filled them with water. After freezing them, he removed the tape, carefully balanced them on measuring cups, spread a variety of materials on top of each icy pie plate, and then diligently recorded how much water dripped through the opening each hour during the winter day. He used his findings to design spreadsheets and graphs. He researched facts about water, ice, and commercial deicers. He used the information to verify his hypothesis. He practiced answering questions a judge might ask at the science fair itself. Not much here that could not be replicated. Nothing really complex.

Scenario #2

Beth's class has chosen an interesting way to study World War II. Instead of reading from a textbook, Beth has asked for eighth-grade volunteers from the community to come in and be interviewed by teams of her eighth grade students about what impact the war had on them, either as military personnel or as civilians.

After careful interviews, the students wrote narratives, took digital photographs, and scanned memorabilia from the time. They looked for Web-based references to the topics and terms they heard about. And finally, they used all this information to create Web pages that allowed them to share what they learned about their neighbors. Both students and teachers worked "overtime" to interview, write, clarify, re-write, and design these pages http://www.isd77.k12.mn.us/schools/ dakota/worldwarII/worldwarIIinterviews.htm).

At an open house, the interviewees and their families were invited in to view and comment on their Web pages. Over 11,000 visitors have read these pages, including many distant family members of those interviewed.

Find below some qualities of LPP (Low Probability of Plagiarism) projects:

1 LPP projects have clarity of purpose and expectations. When Mike started his science fair project, he had a good guide at <www.isd77.k12.mn.us/resources/cf/welcome.html>. On this Web site are also the forms which would be used to judge (assess) his completed project. An understanding of the scientific method including how to form a hypothesis and how to collect supporting data through experimentation and research is clearly stated as the purpose. This is a lifelong, usable set of skills. Science fair students undertake projects worth doing, not just busy work.

2 LPP research projects give students choices. Anyone who has ever attended a science fair has to marvel at the range of topics in which kids are interested. Good projects surround every aspect of every branch of science from chemistry to physics to biology. Now here is the important concept: *If the purpose of the assignment is to teach the scientific method, it doesn't make any difference what the topic is!* Dig down and look at the core concepts your research assignments are trying to teach, and let the students pick specific subjects that interests them.

3 LPP projects are relevant to the student's life. For students, World War II and the Trojan War both just seem "a long time ago." By asking students to interview local residents, the teacher added real faces and lives to history. The stories resonate with those doing the interviewing. So many times we ask our students to research important topics—environmental issues, historical issues, health issues—but fail to help them make the vital connection of why the findings are important to themselves or the people in the town in which they live. The delightful "I-Search" techniques used by Macrorie, Duncan, and Lockhart suggest that "the topic should choose you."

4 LPP projects ask students to write in a narrative rather than an expository style. Beth's students wrote narratives (biographical sketches) rather than simply recording "facts" about WW II, resulting in the research being presented as a narrative of the exploratory process rather than an expository writing project. The "I-Search" techniques also suggest that students write about not just what they discovered, but the story of how they went about gathering their findings.

5 LPP projects stress higher level thinking skills and creativity. Think how different the results of a science project are than a paper that simply asks an "about" question. Hey, Mike, write a research paper about ice. Boring! Instead brainstorm an original theory, design a means of testing it, and find ways to effectively communicate your findings. Suddenly we've moved up on Bloom's taxonomy from the knowledge and inference levels right to application, analysis, synthesis, and evaluation. More fun and impossible to copy.

6 **LPP projects answer real questions.** Mike didn't know at the beginning of his project what really would melt ice the best. His rather creative guess was the laundry detergent (the kind with blue specks) would do the trick. The teacher may have guessed that there was a reason that people pay good money for commercial deicer, but the fact was, he probably did not know either. It was interesting to watch as the experiment's data grew. Beth had no way of knowing the stories the World War II vets would be telling. Their lives were as fresh and exciting to her as they were to her students. Unfortunately, teachers rarely ask questions to which they do not believe they know the answers. Sort of sad, really. Diminishing to the student; boring for the teacher.

The family's role in helping prevent plagiarism:

- Do you help your student develop original, personal opinions and observations as a result of a research project?

- If assigned research does not seem to ask for creative thinking, can you help your student think originally about the material?

- Do you as an adult model and stress the importance of respecting intellectual property?

- Can you help your child understand that it is OK to use a limited amount of the work of others so long as they give credit?

- Do you assist and guide your child's efforts but not complete the work for them?

- Others?

7 **LPP projects involve a variety of information finding activities.** As library media specialists, teachers, and parents, we are comfortable with our familiar old primary sources of reference books, magazine indexes, and trade books. Yet the answers to many personal, local, and timely questions cannot be found in them. They can provide excellent background information, but often we need to talk to experts, conduct surveys, design experiments, or look at other kinds of primary sources to get precise information that is meaningful to the individual. The learners in these examples spent time with secondary sources too, but the generation of new knowledge through hands-on experimentation and primary sources was motivating.

8 **LPP projects tend to be hands-on.** Mike's experiment involved using a hammer to pound nails, a camera to document his progress, a computer to generate charts, and scissors and paste to complete the poster board. Beth's students used tape recorders, scanners, digital cameras, and a Web page construction program. Students are learning by doing, not just by listening. Notice too how many corollary skills were practiced in these "research" projects: writing skills, interviewing skills, photography skills, layout and design skills, and speaking skills.

9 **LPP projects use technology to spur creativity.** Whether for planning, for research, or for communication, many students find the use of technology

What might an LPP project about these topics look like?

States

Diseases

Current Events

Explorers

Presidents

Careers

The Constitution

Nutrition

Simple Machines

Authors

motivating. The challenge of designing containers that make good productivity tools like graphic programs, desktop publishers, and Web page construction kits is virtually the antithesis of copying another's work.

10 LPP projects use formats that use multiple senses. Beth's students were asked to communicate their finds not only with words, but through sound and sight as well. Scanned artifacts like ration coupons, medals, and old photographs stimulated those students who may not be verbal learners. Our ability to digitize and present information is no longer restricted to the written word but now can include drawings, photos, sounds, music, animations, and even movies. All are formats that carry important and often unique information.

11 LPP projects can be complex, but are broken into manageable steps. Mike's science fair project took him over 60 hours to complete and involved dozens of tasks. But early in the project, he and his dad outlined the tasks to be done and established a timeline for their completion. Checking off completed tasks is, in itself, satisfying and motivational, and Mike learned some corollary planning and time management skills in the process. Large projects can be overwhelming even for adults, but planning smaller steps, building timelines, creating frequent deadlines, and scheduling multiple conferences turn complexity into manageability.

12 LPP projects are often collaborative and produce results that are better than individual work. Beth asked her students to work in pairs. Joint problem solving, assigning and accepting responsibility, and discovering and honoring individual talents helped create a synergy that resulted in better, more satisfying Web pages than students working alone would have produced. Not every project needs to be a joint effort, but real-world work environments increasingly stress teamwork. Teamwork in school is not only more enjoyable but leads to the application of practical interpersonal skills as well—and a reduced chance of plagiarism!

13 **LPP projects have results that are shared with people who care and respond.** Science fair participants don't get grades. In Mike's school they don't even get any academic credit. Beth's kids got the same credit as those who took a multiple-choice test on World War II. So why do kids go to all the extra work? I believe kids get hooked because big people take the time to really look at the work they have done and comment on it. Lots of other students all gather on science fair day and share their findings. People take science fair seriously. The community, both physically and virtually, visited the student's World War II Web pages. Assessments and reviews by peers, experts, and neighbors (any audience beyond the teacher) are common in scouting, athletics, dramatics, 4-H, and music organizations. Knowing others will be looking and may detect plagiarism helps reduce its likelihood.

14 **LPP projects are authentically assessed.** Mike was evaluated on his science fair project using a rubric like the one at <www.isd77.k12.mn.us/resources/cf/rubric.htm>. This more closely resembles the criteria used in assessing a person's performance in the real world. Mike and his dad had the rubric at the beginning of the project and used it several times to check his progress during completion of the project. It was easy to recognize both what was good as well as what needed improvement. Quality indicators like rubrics and checklists that are given to students when an assignment is made can help guide learning and keep guesswork to a minimum. As students become more sophisticated in the research process, they should be expected to choose or design their own "rules of quality," one of the indicators of a genuinely intrinsically motivated person.

15 **LPP projects allow the learners to reflect, revisit, revise, and improve their final projects.** While Beth's class had a completion date, students continued to edit and revise their work as they received feedback from those they interviewed and Web site visitors. There is satisfaction to be gained from observed growth. Good projects, like gardens, musical repertoires, and relationships, are probably always works in progress. If students misuse information gathered from another source, they should be given the chance to correct the mistake.

16 **LPP projects are encouraged by adults who believe that given enough time, resources, and motivation, all students are capable of original work.** It's not just the talented and gifted student who can make choices, solve problems creatively, and complete complex tasks. These parents, teachers, and library media specialists know that most students rise to the level of performance expected of them, and that great ideas can come from anyone in the class.

A Research Question Rubric:
Not All Research Questions are Created Equal

Level One: My research is about a broad topic. I can complete the assignment by using a general reference source such as an encyclopedia. I have no personal questions about the topic.

Primary example: My research is about an animal.

Secondary example: My research is about the economy of a state.

Level Two: My research answers a question that helps me narrow the focus of my search. This question may mean that I need to go to various sources to gather enough information to get a reliable answer. The conclusion of the research will ask me to give a supported answer to the question.

Primary example: What methods has my animal developed to help it survive?

Secondary example: What role has manufacturing played in an assigned state's economic development?

Level Three: My research answers a question of personal relevance. To answer this question I may need to consult not just secondary sources such as magazines, newspapers, books, or the Internet, but use primary sources of information such as original surveys, interviews, or source documents.

Primary example: What animal would be best for my family to adopt as a pet?

Secondary example: How can one best prepare for a career in manufacturing in my area?

Level Four: My research answers a personal question about the topic and contains information that may be of use to decision-makers as they make policy or distribute funds. The result of my research is a well-supported conclusion that contains a call for action on the part of an organization or government body. There will be a plan to distribute this information.

Primary example: How can our school help stop the growth in unwanted and abandoned animals in our community?

Secondary example: How might high schools change their curricula to meet the needs of students wanting a career in manufacturing in my state?

Appendix

Glossary

Acceptable Use Policy: a set of guidelines or rules adopted by a school or other organization that governs Internet, network, and information technology use.

Computer crime: a crime committed using a computer, usually to gain access to restricted files, systems, or information. These crimes can resemble trespassing, vandalism, or theft.

Computer virus: a small, intentionally created computer program that causes damage to computer workstations, personal computers, or computer networks. This is a generic term that also includes worms, Trojan horses, and bombs. There have been over 2,000 identified and they are often spread by being attached to files that are sent through networks.

Data privacy: the concept that an individual has a right to say who has personal information about him or her and how that information is used. With the spread of digital information gathering and recordkeeping, data privacy is becoming more difficult to maintain.

Flame: an emotionally, often profane, response to an action or statement in a chatroom, electronic discussion group, or newsgroup.

Hacker/Cracker: an individual who gains unauthorized access to computerized information or computer systems. The term "cracker" implies there is malicious intent to the access.

! **Ethical use** is the most generic term that applies to actions that may be considered right or wrong.

Safe use applies to situations in which physical harm may come to a user or user's property.

Moral use applies to situations to which religious or spiritual values apply. (Is the action good or evil?)

Appropriate use applies to actions which may be right or wrong depending on when, where, and with whom they happen.

Legal use applies to situations in which established laws are violated.

Intellectual property rights: the concept that a person's ideas, writings, and constructions (like computer software) that may not exist in a physical sense should be treated as property and the creators or owners of this property have rights to its sale, use, and control.

Netiquette: a term taken from a combination of "network" and "etiquette" that means a code of polite, thoughtful, or respectful behaviors to be followed while using networks, including the Internet.

Newbie: a new user of networked resources who may not yet know the rules of "netiquette" and runs a risk of being "flamed" for rude behavior.

Peer-to-peer (P2P) file sharing: a type of file sharing that allows computer users with the same program to connect with each other and access files from one another's hard drives rather from a central server. Napster, Gnutella, and KaZaA are examples of peer-to-peer software.

Plagiarism: the use of another's ideas or words as one's own.

Pornography: material, usually of a sexually explicit nature, that is inappropriate for use under certain conditions, such as in a school, with children, where unlawful, or where its presence can be considered a form of harassment.

Spoofing: the use of another's identity when online.

Virtual space: the environment created by computer networks in which data is stored and communication transpires. Also termed "cyberspace."
Virtual spaces often have analogous physical counterparts:

> the virtual library = the library building
> e-mail = physical letters
> chatrooms = coffee shops or salons
> online bookstores = physical bookstores

References

updated version available at <www.doug-johnson.com/ethics>

A selection of my published writings on ethical use issues:

- "Developing Ethical Behaviors in Students: What Schools Must Do." *Educational and Media Technology Yearbook 2003* (forthcoming) <www.doug-johnson.com/dougwri/yearbook.html>.

- "Developing an ethical compass for worlds of learning." *MultiMedia Schools,* Nov/Dec 1998 <www.infotoday.com/MMSchools/nov98/johnson.htm>. (This is the article on which the presentations I give are based.)

- "Copy, cut, plagiarize." *Technology Connection,* January 1996 <www.doug-johnson.com/dougwri/cut.html>.

- "Is it plagiarism?" <www.doug-johnson.com/dougwri/isit.html>.

- "Creating high temptation environments." *Library Talk/The Book Report,* September/October 2000 <www.doug-johnson.com/dougwri/tempt.html>.

- "Mischief and mayhem." *Technology Connection,* December 1997 <www.doug-johnson.com/dougwri/mayhem.html>.

- *Raising good citizens for a virtual world: an online ethics primer for parents.* 2001. Online course for the American Association of School Librarians <www.ala.org/ICONN/fc-ethics.html>.

- "Teacher Webpages That Build Parent Partnerships." *MultiMedia Schools,* September 2000 <www.infotoday.com/MMSchools/sep00/johnson.htm>.

Other published writings on ethical use issues:

- Adams, H. *The Internet Invasion: Is Privacy at Risk?* Follett's Professional Development Series, 2002.

- American Association of School Librarians. 1998. *Information power: building partnerships for learning.* Chicago: American Library Association. (Information literacy standards that address ethical use.)

- Barlow, J. "The Economy of Ideas: A framework for patents and copyrights in the Digital Age." *Wired,* March 1994 <www.wired.com/wired/archive/2.03/economy.ideas.html>.

- Barron, D. "The Library Media Specialist, *Information Power,* and Social Responsibility: Part 1 (Plagiarism)." *School Library Media Activities Monthly,* February 2002.

- Boschmann, E. *The Electronic Classroom: A Handbook for Education in the Electronic Environment.* Learned Information, Inc., 1995.

- Brown, J. "Technology and Ethics." *Learning and Leading with Technology.* March 1997.

- Carpenter, C. "Online Ethics: What's a Teacher to Do?" *Learning and Leading with Technology,* March 1996

- Carter, J. "High Speed High School." *Cable in the Classroom,* June 1998.

- Cohen, Randy. *The Good, the Bad & the Difference: How to Tell the Right from Wrong in Everyday Situations.* (Doubleday, 2002).

- Dyson, E. "Intellectual Value." *Wired,* July 1995 <www.wired.com/wired/archive/3.07/dyson.html>.

- Foss, K. and Lathrop, A. *Student Cheating and Plagiarism in the Internet Era: A Wake-Up Call.* Libraries Unlimited, 2000.

- Gralla, P. *The Complete Idiot's Guide to Protecting Your Children Online.* Que, 2000.

- Harris, R. *The Plagiarism Handbook: Strategies for Preventing, Detecting, and Dealing with Plagiarism.* Pyrczak, 2001.

- Head, S. "Big Brother in a Black Box." *Civilization,* August–September 1999.

- Houston, P. "The Trouble With Ethics." *Sourcebook,* Spring 1991.

- International Society for Technology in Education. 2000. *National educational technology standards for students—connecting curriculum and technology.* Eugene, OR: International Society for Technology in Education. (Technology literacy standards that address ethical use.)

- Johnson, D. G. *Computer Ethics 3rd ed.,* 2000. Paramus, NJ: Prentice-Hall. (Comprehensive and very readable.)

- McEwan, J. "Computer Ethics." *National Institute of Justice Reports,* January–February 1991.

- National Commission on Libraries and Information Science. *Kids and the Internet: the Promise and the Perils* (Practical Guide for Librarians and Library Trustees) brochure, 1998.

- Schwartau W., *Internet & Computer Ethics for Kids (and Parents & Teachers Who Haven't Got a Clue.* Interpact Press, 2001. (Appealing to students. Produced by Nice Kids <www.nicekids.net>.

- Sivin, J and Bialo, E. *Ethical Use of Information Technologies in Education: Important Issues for America's Schools.* U.S. Department of Justice, 1992. (A seminal work.)

- Willard, N. *Computer Ethics, Etiquette & Safety for the 21st-Century Student.* ISTE, 2002. (Great activities for the classroom teacher.)

Web resources on ethical use issues and helpful tools:

- ACM (Association for Computing Machinery) Code of Ethics and Professional Conduct <www.acm.org/constitution/code.html>.

- Alden, S. "Responsible Computing Myths" <www.computerlearning.org/ARTICLES/respmyth.htm>.

- American Civil Liberties Union <www.aclu.org/>.

- American Library Association's "Code of Ethics" <www.ala.org/alaorg/oif/ethics.html>.

- American Library Association's Intellectual Freedom Committee. Questions and Answers on Privacy and Confidentiality <www.ala.org/alaorg/oif/privacyqanda.html>.

- American Library Association's "Privacy: An Interpretation of the Library Bill of Rights" <www.ala.org/alaorg/oif/privacyinterpretation.html>.

- Association of Shareware Professionals <www.asp-shareware.org/>.

- AT&T's Privacy Bird <www.privacybird.com/>.

- Center for Democracy and Privacy <www.cdt.org>.

- Center for Media Education, TeenSites.com. 2001 <www.cme.org>.

- Cody's Science Education Zone <http://ousd.k12.ca.us/~codypren/antidote.html>.

- Computer Ethics (an interactive guide) <http://library.thinkquest.org/26658/>. (Up to date and fun. Part of the larger "ThinkQuest" site.)

- Computer Ethics Institute <www.brook.edu/its/cei/cei_hp.htm>.

- Computer Learning Foundation <http://www.computerlearning.org/respcomp.htm>. (Premier Web site for responsible use of technology by young people. Several articles on this bibliography come from here. Also sells a responsible use curriculum titled "Chip and Friends.")

- Computer Professionals for Social Responsibility <www.cpsr.org/home.html>.

- CONFU Fair Use Guidelines for Educational Media <www.utsystem.edu/OGC/IntellectualProperty/ccmcguid.htm>.

- CyberSmart (curriculum and teacher development) <www.cybersmart.org/home/>.

- Do it yourself: Stop junk mail, e-mail and phone calls <www.obviously.com/junkmail>.

- Electronic Frontier Foundation <www.eff.org>.

- FBI's Parent Guide to Internet Safety <www.fbi.gov/publications/pguide/pguide.htm>.

- Government of Canada. Illegal and Offensive Content on the Internet: the Canadian Strategy to Promote Safe, Wise and Responsible Internet Use. 2002 <http://connect.gc.ca/cyberwise>.

- Harris, R. "Anti-Plagiarism Strategies for Research Papers" <www.virtualsalt.com/antiplag.htm>.

- ID Theft: the U.S. government's central Web site for information about identity theft <www.consumer.gov/idtheft/>.

- Indiana University Bloomington <www.indiana.edu/~wts/wts/plagiarism.html>.

- Internet Privacy Coalition <www.privacy.org/ipc/>.

- Jefferson County (Colorado) copyright chart and guidelines <http://jeffcoweb.jeffco.k12.co.us/plmc/copyright.html>.

- Kabay, M. "The Napster Cantata" <http://networking.earthweb.com/netsysm/article/0,,12089_625221,00.html>.

- Kids Privacy On-line <www.kidsprivacy.com>.

- Lincoln, M. Internet plagiarism: an agenda for staff inservice and student awareness. *MultiMedia Schools*, January/February 2002 <www.infotoday.com/MMSchools/jan02/Lincoln.htm>.

- Lockdown Password FAQ <www.lockdown.co.uk/security/password_faq.php>.

- Magid, L "Filtering Programs Useful But Far From Perfect." SafeKids.com, March 2000 <www.safekids.com/articles/filtering2000.htm>.

- Marsh, M. "Pornography, Plagiarism, Propaganda, Privacy: Teaching Children to Be Responsible Users of Technology Protects Their Rights and the Rights of Others" <www.computerlearning.org/Articles/Ethics98.htm>.

- Meltzer, B. "Digital Photography—a Question of Ethics." *Learning and Leading with Technology*. December-January 1995-96 <www.fno.org/may97/digital.html>.

- National Center for Missing and Exploited Children Web site <www.missingkids.com/>.

- National Crime Prevention Council's "Preventing Vandalism" <www.ncpc.org/2vandals.htm>.

- Nice Kids: Network for Internet and Computer Ethics <www.nicekids.net>.

- North Central Regional Education Laboratory "Technology Resource Usage Policy Template" <www.ncrel.org/tplan/handbook/toolkt12.htm>.

- Pew Internet & American Life Project "Teenage Life Online" <www.pewinternet.org/reports>.

- Purdue University Online Writing Lab (OWL) Avoiding Plagiarism <http://owl.english.purdue.edu/handouts/research/r_plagiar.html>.

- Queensland (Australia) Department of Education. Web publishing for schools (draft). 2002 <http://education.qld.gov.au/corporate/publishing/internet/html/guidelines/schools/>.

- Responsible Netizen <http://netizen.uoregon.edu>.

- Rinaldi, A. "The Net: User Guidelines and Netiquette" <www.fau.edu/netiquette/net/>.

- SafeKids.com <www.safekids.com>.

- Scambusters <www.scambusters.org/>.

- Schools Sucks <www.schoolsucks.com>. (Repository of downloadable term papers.)

- Schrock, K. "Critical Evaluation Information" (of Web sites) <http://school.discovery.com/schrockguide/eval.html>.

- Sherwood, K. A Beginner's Guide to Effective Email <www.webfoot.com/advice/email.top.html>.

- Software & Industry Information Association (formerly the Software Publishers Association) <www.spa.org>.

- Strategies for Teaching Children Responsible Use of Technology <www.computerlearning.org/ARTICLES/ethictch.htm>.

- Templeton, B. "10 Big Myths about Copyright Explained" <www.templetons.com/brad/copymyths.html>.

- Turnitin <www.turnitin.com>.

- United States Department of Education. "Parents Guide to the Internet." November 1997 <www.ed.gov/pubs/parents/internet/>.

- United States Department of Energy's CIAC Information Bulletin I-034 Internet Cookies <http://ciac.llnl.gov/ciac/bulletins/i-034.shtml>.

- United States Department of Energy. Hoaxbusters <hoaxbusters.ciac.org/>.

- Valenza, J. "Teaching Ethics in a World of Electronics." *Philadelphia Inquirer*, March 18, 1999 <http://joycevalenza.com/ethics.html>.

- Yahoo! Briefcase <briefcase.yahoo.com>.

Ethics Questionnaire I

Privacy

1 John fills out a survey form on a computer game Web page. The survey asks for his e-mail address, mailing address, and telephone number, which he fills in. In the following weeks, he receives several advertisements in the mail as well as dozens of e-mail messages about new computer games. Is what John did:

☐ Right

☐ Wrong

☐ Sometimes right and sometimes wrong depending on the situation

☐ I don't know

2 Adele "meets" Frank, who shares her interest in figure skating, in an Internet chatroom. After several conversations in the following weeks, Frank asks Adele for her home telephone number and address. Adele likes Frank and gives him the information he asked for. Is what Adele did:

☐ Right

☐ Wrong

☐ Sometimes right and sometimes wrong depending on the situation

☐ I don't know

3 The principal suspects Paul of using his school e-mail account to send offensive messages to other students. He asks the network manager to give him copies of Paul's e-mail. What the principal has done is:

☐ Right

☐ Wrong

☐ Sometimes right and sometimes wrong depending on the situation

☐ I don't know

4 Jennie's sister needs to leave the computer to take laundry from the dryer. While she is gone, Jennie finds she has been working on an e-mail to her best friend and that her e-mail program is still open. She checks to see what sis has to say. Are Jennie's actions:

☐ Right

☐ Wrong

☐ Sometimes right and sometimes wrong depending on the situation

☐ I don't know

5 Ms. West, Terry's teacher, needs to leave the room to take care of an emergency. While she is gone, Terry finds that Ms. West had been working on student progress reports and that her grading program is still open on her computer. He checks to see what grade he is getting and finds the grades for several other students. What Terry did is:

☐ Right

☐ Wrong

☐ Sometimes right and sometimes wrong depending on the situation

☐ I don't know

6 Alfreda received an unsolicited e-mail in her student account for a product. Included in the e-mail was an e-mail address she could respond to if she did not wish to receive any additional e-mail from this company. After replying, the volume of spam in her account increased dramatically. What Alfreda did is:

☐ Right

☐ Wrong

☐ Sometimes right and sometimes wrong depending on the situation

☐ I don't know

7 Mr. Black, the school library media specialist, posts lists of overdue materials on the school Intranet. The lists include student names and titles of the materials. Clarice is upset by this policy and asks the principal how it can be changed. What Clarice did is:

- ☐ Right
- ☐ Wrong
- ☐ Sometimes right and sometimes wrong depending on the situation
- ☐ I don't know

8 Joel shared his password for his e-mail network access account with his buddy Lyle. He has found that several documents are missing from his online storage space. What Joel did is:

- ☐ Right
- ☐ Wrong
- ☐ Sometimes right and sometimes wrong depending on the situation
- ☐ I don't know

9 While the teacher was out of the room, Trixie decided to visit a site that she knew violated the school and classroom rules. The next day, the teacher brought Trixie and her parents in for a conference. A program on the computer she was using logged the Internet sites she visited. Trixie felt her privacy had been violated. Are Trixie's feelings:

- ☐ Justfied
- ☐ Not justified
- ☐ Sometimes justified and sometimes not justified depending on the situation
- ☐ I don't know

10 Ike and Tina created a Web page to meet the requirements of a school assignment. On the Web page they included their pictures and e-mail addresses hoping to get feedback on their page. Were Ike and Tina's actions:

- ☐ Right
- ☐ Wrong
- ☐ Sometimes right and sometimes wrong depending on the situation
- ☐ I don't know

11 Anne has a credit card with the permission of her parents. She finds a music CD that is not available locally on a Web site. She fills in the online order form with her name, address, telephone number, and credit card account number and hits the "submit" button. What Anne did is:

- ☐ Right
- ☐ Wrong
- ☐ Sometimes right and sometimes wrong depending on the situation
- ☐ I don't know

12 In Sun-Kim's house the computer with Internet access is in the family room. Sun-Kim has been lobbying her mother to let her have a computer with Internet access in her room since her younger brothers often make it difficult for her to concentrate while she is online. Would allowing Sun-Kim to have a Internet access in her room be:

- ☐ Right
- ☐ Wrong
- ☐ Sometimes right and sometimes wrong depending on the situation
- ☐ I don't know

Property

13 Jerry borrows Ben's game disks for *Monster Truck Rally II* and installs them on his home computer. He says he will erase the game if he does not like it, or will buy the game for himself if he likes it. Jerry has been using the game now for over a month and has not erased it from his computer and has not bought his own copy. Is Jerry's use of the game:

☐ Right

☐ Wrong

☐ Sometimes right and sometimes wrong depending on the situation

☐ I don't know

14 Betty downloads a solitaire card game from the Internet that is "shareware." It can be legally used for 30 days and then Betty must either delete it from her computer or send its author a fee. Betty has been using the game for 30 days. Is Betty's use of the game:

☐ Right

☐ Wrong

☐ Sometimes right and sometimes wrong depending on the situation

☐ I don't know

15 Cindy finds some good information about plant growth nutrients for her science fair project on a CD-ROM reference title. She uses the copy function of the computer to take an entire paragraph from the CD-ROM article and paste it directly into her report. She writes down the title of the article and the CD-ROM from which it was taken. When she writes her report, she provides a citation and lists the source in her bibliography. Are Cindy's actions:

☐ Right

☐ Wrong

☐ Sometimes right and sometimes wrong depending on the situation

☐ I don't know

16 Albert finds a site on the Internet that is a collection of old term papers for students to read and use. He downloads one on ancient Greece, changes the title, and submits it as his own. How Albert completed the assignment is:

☐ Right

☐ Wrong

☐ Sometimes right and sometimes wrong depending on the situation

☐ I don't know

17 Fahad is upset with his friend George. He finds the data disk on which George has been storing his essays and erases it. Are Fahad's actions:

☐ Right

☐ Wrong

☐ Sometimes right and sometimes wrong depending on the situation

☐ I don't know

18 Lucy uses the family computer to download a program from the Internet that has instructions on how to make paper airplanes. After using the program, the computer does not seem to work very well, crashing often and randomly destroying files. Lucy thinks she might have downloaded a virus along with the paper airplane program. Are Lucy's actions:

☐ Right

☐ Wrong

☐ Sometimes right and sometimes wrong depending on the situation

☐ I don't know

19 Henry's older friend Hank, a high school student, has discovered the password to the school's student information system. Because Hank feels a teacher has unfairly given him a poor grade, he plans to create a "bomb" which will erase all the information on the office computer. Henry tells his dad about Hank's plan. Are Henry's actions:

☐ Right
☐ Wrong
☐ Sometimes right and sometimes wrong depending on the situation
☐ I don't know

20 Brady has been taking advantage of a Napster-like peer-to-peer service to download all his favorite songs, save them on his hard drive, and load them to his MP3 player. He can cite articles that show the sales of music CDs have actually risen as a result of music "swapping" on the Internet. Are Brady's actions:

☐ Right
☐ Wrong
☐ Sometimes right and sometimes wrong depending on the situation
☐ I don't know

21 Sara has begun working and has some money she would like to invest. She receives an e-mail that promises a 500% return on her investment. She sends the company a check for $200. Are Sara's actions:

☐ Right
☐ Wrong
☐ Sometimes right and sometimes wrong depending on the situation
☐ I don't know

22 Raul is creating a videotape for his History Day project. As background music he is using Billy Joel's song "We Didn't Start the Fire" that he has digitized from a CD he owns. The song works well for his exploration of the causes of global conflict. The projects will compete initially within his school and winners will advance to regional competitions. Are Raul's actions:

☐ Right
☐ Wrong
☐ Sometimes right and sometimes wrong depending on the situation
☐ I don't know

23 Barry is very careful about not plagiarizing. When using information from the online encyclopedia, he is careful about changing at least a few words in each sentence. Are Barry's actions:

☐ Right
☐ Wrong
☐ Sometimes right and sometimes wrong depending on the situation
☐ I don't know

24 Benita is rightfully proud of her personal Internet site. She has found pictures, cartoons, and sayings on the Web and copied them to her site. She links to lots of other favorite sites. When asked if her use of items she has found on the Web might violate copyright, she replied that she was careful to use only those things that did not have a copyright notice. Is Benita's use of these items:

☐ Right
☐ Wrong
☐ Sometimes right and sometimes wrong depending on the situation
☐ I don't know

a(P)propriate use

25 Jack's class has been using the digital camera to take pictures for the school year book. Jack has found that he can use a computer program to change the photographs. He has used the program so far to make himself look like the tallest boy in the class, to blacken out the front tooth of his best buddy who will think it is funny, and to give his teacher slightly crossed eyes. Are Jack's actions:

☐ Right
☐ Wrong
☐ Sometimes right and sometimes wrong depending on the situation
☐ I don't know

26 Just for fun, thirteen-year-old Alice tells the other people on her electronic mailing list that she is twenty years old and a nursing student. Others on the list have begun e-mailing her health-related questions. Are Alice's actions:

☐ Right
☐ Wrong
☐ Sometimes right and sometimes wrong depending on the situation
☐ I don't know

27 Penelope has found a Web site that has "gross jokes" on it. She prints the pages and shares them with her friends. Are Penelope's actions:

☐ Right
☐ Wrong
☐ Sometimes right and sometimes wrong depending on the situation
☐ I don't know

28 The computers in the library always seem to be busy. Otis tells the librarian he is working on a research project, but actually uses the computer to access the latest soccer scores posted on the Internet. Are Otis's actions:

☐ Right
☐ Wrong
☐ Sometimes right and sometimes wrong depending on the situation
☐ I don't know

29 Just for fun, Nellie sets the print command on her computer to print 50 copies of an electronic encyclopedia article she's been reading, and then walks away. Are Nellie's actions:

☐ Right
☐ Wrong
☐ Sometimes right and sometimes wrong depending on the situation
☐ I don't know

30 As a joke, Chang sends an e-mail message to his sister who attends a school across town. In this e-mail he uses profanities and racial slurs. Are Chang's actions:

☐ Right
☐ Wrong
☐ Sometimes right and sometimes wrong depending on the situation
☐ I don't know

31 Clark downloads a page with sexually explicit photographs from the Internet to a computer in the classroom. He shows its contents to others in his class. Are Clark's actions:

☐ Right
☐ Wrong
☐ Sometimes right and sometimes wrong depending on the situation
☐ I don't know

32 Linda suffers from an eating disorder. She has been accessing "pro-anorexia" sites on the Internet and participating in chats with other young people who share her condition in order to get support for the continuation of her behaviors. Are Linda's actions:

- ☐ Right
- ☐ Wrong
- ☐ Sometimes right and sometimes wrong depending on the situation
- ☐ I don't know

33 All the students at Peter and Paul's school have been given PDAs (personal digital assistants—small, handheld computers). The boys have been using the wireless transmission features to exchange notes and test answers in class. Are the boys' actions:

- ☐ Right
- ☐ Wrong
- ☐ Sometimes right and sometimes wrong depending on the situation
- ☐ I don't know

34 Bill has created an "alternative" school Web site on a commercial server. His site satirizes school activities, holds doctored photos of staff members, and makes fun of fellow students. When the principal discovers the Web site, he withdraws the recommendation he has written for a college scholarship for which Bill has applied. Are Bill's actions:

- ☐ Right
- ☐ Wrong
- ☐ Sometimes right and sometimes wrong depending on the situation
- ☐ I don't know

35 Debbie is running for class president. She uses an electronic mailing list (listserv) to send regular e-mails to all the students in her class explaining her platform and actions she would take as president. Are Debbie's actions:

- ☐ Right
- ☐ Wrong
- ☐ Sometimes right and sometimes wrong depending on the situation
- ☐ I don't know

36 Alex is observed by the library media specialist accessing "adult" sites. When asked about his choice of sites, he readily admits that he has chosen to do his senior thesis on Internet pornography. Are Alex's actions:

- ☐ Right
- ☐ Wrong
- ☐ Sometimes right and sometimes wrong depending on the situation
- ☐ I don't know

Permission is freely given for teachers to use this material with students as long as credit to the source is given. I welcome comments about your students' responses.

Doug Johnson
<dougj@doug-johnson.com>
<www.doug-johnson.com>

Ethics Questionnaire II

Privacy

1 John fills out a survey form in a computer magazine. The survey asks for his mailing address, and telephone number, which he fills in. In the following weeks, he receives several advertisements in the mail as well as dozens of telephone solicitations about new computer games. Is what John did:

- ☐ Right
- ☐ Wrong
- ☐ Sometimes right and sometimes wrong depending on the situation
- ☐ I don't know

2 Adele meets Frank, who shares her interest in figure skating, at the shopping center. After several conversations in the following weeks, Frank asks Adele for her home telephone number and address. Adele likes Frank and gives him the information he asked for. Is what Adele did:

- ☐ Right
- ☐ Wrong
- ☐ Sometimes right and sometimes wrong depending on the situation
- ☐ I don't know

3 The principal suspects Paul of writing offensive notes to other students. He asks the custodian for a key to Paul's locker so he can read through his notebooks. What the principal has done is:

- ☐ Right
- ☐ Wrong
- ☐ Sometimes right and sometimes wrong depending on the situation
- ☐ I don't know

4 Jennie's sister needs to leave her diary on the coffee table to take laundry from the dryer. While she is gone, Jennie checks to see what sis has to say. Are Jennie's actions:

- ☐ Right
- ☐ Wrong
- ☐ Sometimes right and sometimes wrong depending on the situation
- ☐ I don't know

5 Ms. West, Terry's teacher, needs to leave the room to take care of an emergency. While she is gone, Terry finds that Ms. West left her grade book open on her desk. He checks to see what grade he is getting and looks at the grades for several other students. What Terry did is:

- ☐ Right
- ☐ Wrong
- ☐ Sometimes right and sometimes wrong depending on the situation
- ☐ I don't know

6 Alfreda received an unsolicited catalog for products of an adult nature in the mail at home. Receiving this material has made her feel uncomfortable. She called the company, asking to be removed from its mailing list. What Alfreda did is:

- ☐ Right
- ☐ Wrong
- ☐ Sometimes right and sometimes wrong depending on the situation
- ☐ I don't know

7 Mr. Black, the school library media specialist, posts lists of overdue materials on the bulletin board outside the media center. The lists include student names and titles of the materials. Clarice is upset by this policy and asks the principal how it can be changed. What Clarice did is:

- [ ] Right
- [ ] Wrong
- [ ] Sometimes right and sometimes wrong depending on the situation
- [ ] I don't know

8 Joel shared his locker combination with his buddy Lyle. He has found that several books are missing from the locker. What Joel did is:

- [ ] Right
- [ ] Wrong
- [ ] Sometimes right and sometimes wrong depending on the situation
- [ ] I don't know

8 While the bus driver wasn't looking, Trixie decided to throw a paper wad at another student, an action that she knew violated the school and bus rules. The next day, the teacher brought Trixie and her parents in for a conference. A video camera on the bus showed her throwing the paper. Trixie felt her privacy had been violated. Were Trixie's feelings:

- [ ] Right
- [ ] Wrong
- [ ] Sometimes right and sometimes wrong depending on the situation
- [ ] I don't know

10 Ike and Tina wrote a newsletter to meet the requirements of a school assignment. In the newsletter, which they distributed through the school and town, they included their pictures and phone numbers hoping to get feedback on their writing. Were Ike and Tina's actions:

- [ ] Right
- [ ] Wrong
- [ ] Sometimes right and sometimes wrong depending on the situation
- [ ] I don't know

11 Anne has a credit card with the permission of her parents. In a catalog with a toll-free telephone number, she finds a music CD that is not available locally. She gives the operator who answers the call her name, address, telephone number, and credit card account number to complete the order. What Anne did is:

- [ ] Right
- [ ] Wrong
- [ ] Sometimes right and sometimes wrong depending on the situation
- [ ] I don't know

12 In Sun-Kim's house the telephone and encyclopedias are in the family room. Sun-Kim has been lobbying her mother to let her have telephone access in her room and move the encyclopedias there as well since her younger brothers often make it difficult for her to concentrate. Would allowing Sun-Kim to have a telephone and the encyclopedias in her room be:

- [ ] Right
- [ ] Wrong
- [ ] Sometimes right and sometimes wrong depending on the situation
- [ ] I don't know

Property

13 Jerry borrows Ben's comic book *Monster Truck Rally II* and photocopies it. He says he will throw the copy away after he's read it or will buy the comic for himself if he likes it. Jerry has had the copied comic now for over a month and has not thrown it away and has not bought his own copy. Is Jerry's use of the comic:

- ☐ Right
- ☐ Wrong
- ☐ Sometimes right and sometimes wrong depending on the situation
- ☐ I don't know

14 Betty orders a "free trial version" of a solitaire card game. It can be legally used for 30 days and then Betty must either pay for it or return it. Betty has been using the game for 30 days. Is Betty's use of the game:

- ☐ Right
- ☐ Wrong
- ☐ Sometimes right and sometimes wrong depending on the situation
- ☐ I don't know

15 Cindy finds some good information about plant growth nutrients for her science fair in an encyclopedia. She copies an entire paragraph from the encyclopedia article directly into her report. She writes down the title of the article and the encyclopedia from which it was taken. When she writes her report, she cites the paragraph, and lists the source in her bibliography. Are Cindy's actions:

- ☐ Right
- ☐ Wrong
- ☐ Sometimes right and sometimes wrong depending on the situation
- ☐ I don't know

16 Albert tells his older brother he has to write a report on ancient Greece. His brother trades him a report that he wrote two years ago for the same class for a t-shirt. Albert recopies the report, changes the title, and submits it as his own. How Albert completed the assignment is:

- ☐ Right
- ☐ Wrong
- ☐ Sometimes right and sometimes wrong depending on the situation
- ☐ I don't know

17 Fahad is upset with his friend George. He finds the notebook in which George has been writing his essays and tears out all the pages with writing. Are Fahad's actions:

- ☐ Right
- ☐ Wrong
- ☐ Sometimes right and sometimes wrong depending on the situation
- ☐ I don't know

18 Lucy visits a friend who is not feeling well. A few days later, Lucy and her brother get a rash and headache. Lucy's friend had the chicken pox. Are Lucy's actions:

- ☐ Right
- ☐ Wrong
- ☐ Sometimes right and sometimes wrong depending on the situation
- ☐ I don't know

19 Henry's older friend Hank, a high school student, has found a key to the school's office. Because Hank feels a teacher has unfairly given him a poor grade, he plans to sneak in at night and destroy all the student records. Henry tells his dad about Hank's plan. By reporting Hank, is Henry:

- ☐ Right
- ☐ Wrong
- ☐ Sometimes right and sometimes wrong depending on the situation
- ☐ I don't know

20 Brady has been taping songs off the radio and from CDs he has borrowed from his friends. Are Brady's actions:

- ☐ Right
- ☐ Wrong
- ☐ Sometimes right and sometimes wrong depending on the situation
- ☐ I don't know

21 Sara has begun working and has some money she would like to invest. She receives a flyer in the mail that promises a 500% return on her investment. She sends the company a check for $200. Are Sara's actions:

- ☐ Right
- ☐ Wrong
- ☐ Sometimes right and sometimes wrong depending on the situation
- ☐ I don't know

22 Raul is creating a newspaper for his History Day project. He has used photocopies of photographs from library books to help illustrate his stories. The projects will compete initially within his school and winners will advance to regional competitions. Are Raul's actions:

- ☐ Right
- ☐ Wrong
- ☐ Sometimes right and sometimes wrong depending on the situation
- ☐ I don't know

23 Barry is very careful about not plagiarizing. When using information from a magazine, he is careful about changing at least a few words in each sentence. Are Barry's actions:

- ☐ Right
- ☐ Wrong
- ☐ Sometimes right and sometimes wrong depending on the situation
- ☐ I don't know

24 Benita is rightfully proud of the inside of her locker. She made photocopies of pictures, cartoons, and sayings in magazines and has taped them to the locker. When asked if her use of items she has found in magazines might violate copyright, she replied that she was careful to use only those things that did not have a copyright notice. Is Benita's use of these items:

- ☐ Right
- ☐ Wrong
- ☐ Sometimes right and sometimes wrong depending on the situation
- ☐ I don't know

a(P)propriate use

25 Jack's class has been using the camera to take pictures for the school yearbook. Jack has found that he can change the photographs if he draws on them carefully. He blackens out the front tooth of his best friend, who thinks it is funny, and gives his teacher slightly crossed eyes. Are Jack's actions:

- ☐ Right
- ☐ Wrong
- ☐ Sometimes right and sometimes wrong depending on the situation
- ☐ I don't know

26 Just for fun, thirteen-year-old Alice calls into a radio talk show and says that she is twenty years old and a nursing student. She offers some health-related advice. Are Alice's actions:

- ☐ Right
- ☐ Wrong
- ☐ Sometimes right and sometimes wrong depending on the situation
- ☐ I don't know

27 Penelope has a book with "gross jokes" in it. She brings the book to school and shares the jokes with her friends. Are Penelope's actions:

- ☐ Right
- ☐ Wrong
- ☐ Sometimes right and sometimes wrong depending on the situation
- ☐ I don't know

28 The tables in the library always seem to be full. Otis tells the librarian he is working on a research project, but actually uses his time in the library to read *Sports Illustrated*. Are Otis's actions:

- ☐ Right
- ☐ Wrong
- ☐ Sometimes right and sometimes wrong depending on the situation
- ☐ I don't know

29 Just for fun, Nellie sets the print command on the photocopier to print 50 copies of an article she's been reading, and then walks away. Are Nellie's actions:

- ☐ Right
- ☐ Wrong
- ☐ Sometimes right and sometimes wrong depending on the situation
- ☐ I don't know

30 As a joke, Chang calls his sister who attends a school across town. During the call, he uses profanities and racial slurs. Are Chang's actions:

- ☐ Right
- ☐ Wrong
- ☐ Sometimes right and sometimes wrong depending on the situation
- ☐ I don't know

31 Clark brings a copy of his dad's *Penthouse* magazine to school. He shows its contents to others in his class. Are Clark's actions:

- ☐ Right
- ☐ Wrong
- ☐ Sometimes right and sometimes wrong depending on the situation
- ☐ I don't know

32 Linda suffers from an eating disorder. She has been meeting at a local coffee house with other young people who share her condition in order to get support for the continuation of her behaviors. Are Linda's actions:

- ☐ Right
- ☐ Wrong
- ☐ Sometimes right and sometimes wrong depending on the situation
- ☐ I don't know

33 Peter and Paul have been passing notes in class and devising schemes to share answers in class using a set of hand signals. Are the boys' actions:

- ☐ Right
- ☐ Wrong
- ☐ Sometimes right and sometimes wrong depending on the situation
- ☐ I don't know

34 Bill has created an "alternative" school newspaper that he sells off school grounds. His paper satirizes school activities, holds doctored photos of staff members, and makes fun of fellow students. When the principal discovers the newspaper, he withdraws the recommendation he has written for a college scholarship for which Bill has applied. Are Bill's actions:

- ☐ Right
- ☐ Wrong
- ☐ Sometimes right and sometimes wrong depending on the situation
- ☐ I don't know

35 Debbie is running for class president. She makes posters and hangs them on the walls of the school and on student lockers. Her campaign committee calls students at home and sends "elect Debbie" messages to their pagers. Are Debbie's actions:

☐ Right

☐ Wrong

☐ Sometimes right and sometimes wrong depending on the situation

☐ I don't know

36 Alex is observed by the library media specialist reading "adult" novels. When asked about his choice of reading material, he readily admits that he has chosen to do his senior thesis on the history of pornography. Are Alex's actions:

☐ Right

☐ Wrong

☐ Sometimes right and sometimes wrong depending on the situation

☐ I don't know

Permission is freely given for teachers to use this material with students as long as credit to the source is given. I welcome comments about your students' responses.

Doug Johnson
<dougj@doug-johnson.com>
<www.doug-johnson.com>

Sample

Internet Acceptable Use Policy

(from the Mankato (Minnesota) Area Public Schools, ISD77)

Adopted: *Date* Policy Number
Revised: *Date*

I. PURPOSE

The purpose of this policy is to set forth policies and guidelines for access to the school district computer system and acceptable and safe use of the Internet, including electronic communications.

II. GENERAL STATEMENT OF POLICY

In making decisions regarding student access to the school district computer system and the Internet, including electronic communications, the school district considers its own stated educational mission, goals, and objectives. Electronic information research skills are now fundamental to preparation of citizens and future employees. Access to the school district computer system and to the Internet enables students to explore thousands of libraries, databases, bulletin boards, and other resources while exchanging messages with people around the world. The school district expects that faculty will blend thoughtful use of the school district computer system and the Internet throughout the curriculum and will provide guidance and instruction to students in their use.

III. LIMITED EDUCATIONAL PURPOSE

The school district is providing students and employees with access to the school district's computer system, which includes Internet access. The purpose of the system more specific than providing students and employees with general access to the Internet. The school district system has a limited educational purpose, which includes use of the system for classroom activities, professional or career development, and limited high-quality, self-discovery activities. Users are expected to use Internet access through the district system to further educational and personal goals consistent with the mission of the school district and school policies. Uses which might be acceptable on a user's private personal account on another system may not be acceptable on this limited purpose network.

VI. USE OF SYSTEM IS A PRIVILEGE

The use of the school district system and access to use of the Internet is a privilege, not a right. Depending on the nature and degree of the violation and the number of previous violations, unacceptable use of the school district system or the Internet may result in one or more of the following consequences: suspension or cancellation of use of access privileges; payments for damages and repairs; discipline under other appropriate school district policies, including suspension, expulsion, exclusion or termination of employment; or civil or criminal liability under other applicable laws.

V. UNACCEPTABLE USES

A. The following uses of the school district system and Internet resources or accounts are considered unacceptable:

1. Users will not use the school district system to access, review, upload, download, store, print, post, or distribute pornographic, obscene or sexually explicit material or other visual depictions that are harmful to minors.

2. Users will not use the school district system to transmit or receive obscene, abusive, profane, lewd, vulgar, rude, inflammatory, threatening, disrespectful, or sexually explicit language.

3. Users will not use the school district system to access, review, upload, download, store, print, post, or distribute materials that use language or images that are inappropriate to the educational setting or disruptive to the educational process and will not post information or materials that could cause damage or danger of disruption.

4. Users will not use the school district system to access, review, upload, download, store, print, post, or distribute materials that use language or images that advocate violence or discrimination toward other people (hate literature) or that may constitute harassment or discrimination.

5. Users will not use the school district system to knowingly or recklessly post false or defamatory information about a person or organization, or to harass another person, or to engage in personal attacks, including prejudicial or discriminatory attacks.

6. Users will not use the school district system to engage in any illegal act or violate any local, state, or federal statute or law.

7. Users will not use the school district system to vandalize, damage, or disable the property of another person or organization, will not make deliberate attempts to degrade or disrupt equipment, software or system performance by spreading computer viruses or by any other means, will not tamper with, modify or change the school district system software, hardware or wiring or take any action to violate the school district system's security, and will not use the school district system in such a way as to disrupt the use of the system by other users.

8. Users will not use the school district system to gain unauthorized access to information resources or to access another person's materials, information, or files without the implied or direct permission of that person.

9. Users will not use the school district system to post private information about another person, personal contact information about themselves or other persons, or other personally identifiable information, including but not limited to, home addresses, telephone numbers, identification numbers, account numbers, access codes or passwords, labeled photographs or other information that would make the individual's identity easily traceable, and will not repost a message that was sent to the user privately without permission of the person who sent the message.

10. Users will not attempt to gain unauthorized access to the school district system or any other system through the school district system, attempt to log in through another person's account, or use computer accounts, access codes, or network identification other than those assigned to the user.

11. Users will not use the school district system to violate copyright laws, or usage licensing agreements, or otherwise to use another person's property without the person's prior approval or proper citation, including the downloading or exchanging of pirated software or copying software to or from any school computer, and will not plagiarize works they find on the Internet.

12. Users will not use the school district system for the conduct of a business, for unauthorized commercial purposes or for financial gain unrelated to the mission of the school district. Users will not use the school district system to offer or provide goods or services or for product advertisement. Users will not use the school district system to purchase goods or services for personal use without authorization from the appropriate school district official.

B. If a user inadvertently accesses unacceptable materials or an unacceptable Internet site, the user shall immediately disclose the inadvertent access to an appropriate school district official. This disclosure may serve as a defense against an allegation that the user has intentionally violated this policy. A user may also in certain rare instances access otherwise unacceptable materials if necessary to complete an assignment and if done with the prior approval of and with appropriate guidance from the appropriate teacher.

VI. FILTER

    A. With respect to any of its computers with Internet access, the school district will monitor the online activities of minors and employ technology protection measures during any use of such computers by minors and adults. The technology protection measures utilized will monitor material deemed:

        1. Obscene

        2. Child pornography; or

        3. Harmful to minors.

    B. The term "harmful to minors" means any picture, image, graphic image file, or other visual depiction that:

        1. taken as a whole and with respect to minors, appeals to a prurient interest in nudity, sex, or excretion; or

        2. depicts, describes, or represents, in a patently offensive way with respect to what is suitable for minors, an actual or simulated sexual act or sexual contact, actual or simulated normal or perverted sexual acts, or a lewd exhibition of the genitals; and

        3. taken as a whole, lacks serious literary, artistic, political, or scientific value as to minors.

    C. An administrator, supervisor, or other person authorized by the Superintendent may disable the technology protection measure, during use by an adult, to enable access for bona fide research or other lawful purposes.

VII. CONSISTENCY WITH OTHER SCHOOL POLICIES

Use of the school district computer system and use of the Internet shall be consistent with school district policies and the mission of the school district.

VIII. LIMITED EXPECTATION OF PRIVACY

    A. By authorizing use of the school district system, the school district does not relinquish control over materials on the system or contained in files on the system. Users should expect only limited privacy in the contents of personal files on the school district system.

    B. Routine maintenance and monitoring of the school district system may lead to a discovery that a user has violated this policy, another school district policy, or the law.

    C. An individual investigation or search will be conducted if school authorities have a reasonable suspicion that the search will uncover a violation of law or school district policy.

    D. Parents have the right at any time to investigate or review the contents of their child's files and e-mail files. Parents have the right to request the termination of their child's individual accounts at any time.

E. School district employees should be aware that data and other materials in files maintained on the school district system may be subject to review, disclosure, or discovery under Minnesota Statutes, Chapter 13 (the Minnesota Government Data Practices Act).

F. The school district will cooperate fully with local, state, and federal authorities in any investigation concerning or related to any illegal activities and activities not in compliance with school district policies conducted through the school district system.

IX. INTERNET USE AGREEMENT

A. The proper use of the Internet, and the educational value to be gained from proper Internet use, is the joint responsibility of students, parents, and employees of the school district.

B. This policy requires the permission of and supervision by the school's designated professional staff before a student may use a school account or resource to access the Internet.

C. The Internet Use Agreement form must be read and signed by the user and the parent or guardian. The form must then be filed at the school office.

X. LIMITATION ON SCHOOL DISTRICT LIABILITY

Use of the school district system is at the user's own risk. The system is provided on an "as is, as available" basis. The school district will not be responsible for any damage users may suffer, including, but not limited to, loss, damage or unavailability of data stored on school district diskettes, tapes, hard drives or servers, or for delays or changes in or interruptions of service or misdeliveries or nondeliveries of information or materials, regardless of the cause. The school district is not responsible for the accuracy or quality of any advice or information obtained through or stored on the school district system. The school district will not be responsible for financial obligations arising through unauthorized use of the school district system or the Internet.

XI. USER NOTIFICATION

A. All users shall be notified of the school district policies relating to Internet use.

B. This notification shall include the following:

1. Notification that Internet use is subject to compliance with school district policies.

2. Disclaimers limiting the school district's liability relative to

a. Information stored on school district diskettes, hard drives, or servers.

b. Information retrieved through school district computers, networks, or online resources.

c. Personal property used to access school district computers, networks, or online resources.

d. Unauthorized financial obligations resulting from use of school district resources/accounts to access the Internet.

3. A description of the privacy rights and limitations of school sponsored/managed Internet accounts.

4. Notification that, even though the school district may use technical means to limit student Internet access, these limits do not provide a foolproof means for enforcing the provisions of this acceptable use policy.

5. Notification that goods and services can be purchased over the Internet that could potentially result in unwanted financial obligations and that any financial obligation incurred by a student through the Internet is the sole responsibility of the student or the student's parents.

6. Notification that the collection, creation, reception, maintenance, and dissemination of data via the Internet, including electronic communications, is governed by Policy 406, Public and Private Personnel Data, and Policy 515, Protection and Privacy of Pupil Records.

7. Notification that should the user violate the school district's acceptable use policy, the student's access privileges may be revoked, school disciplinary action may be taken and/or appropriate legal action may be taken.

8. Notification that all provisions of the acceptable use policy are subordinate to local, state, and federal laws.

XII. PARENT RESPONSIBILITY; NOTIFICATION OF STUDENT INTERNET USE

A. Outside of school, parents bear responsibility for the same guidance of Internet use as they exercise with information sources such as television, telephones, radio, movies, and other possibly offensive media. Parents are responsible for monitoring their students' uses of the school district system and of the Internet if the students are accessing the school district system from home or a remote location.

B. Parents will be notified that their students will be using school district resources/accounts to access the Internet and that the school district will provide parents the option to request alternative activities not requiring Internet access. This notification should include:

1. A copy of the user notification form provided to the student user.

2. A description of parent/guardian responsibilities.

3. A statement that the Internet Use Agreement must be signed by the user, the parent or guardian, and a supervising teacher prior to use by the student.

4. A statement that the school district's acceptable use policy is available for parental review.

XIII. IMPLEMENTATION; POLICY REVIEW

A. The school district administration may develop appropriate guidelines and procedures necessary to implement this policy for submission to the school board for approval. Upon approval by the school board, such guidelines and procedures shall be an addendum to this policy.

B. The administration shall revise the student and parent notifications, if necessary, to reflect the adoption of these guidelines and procedures.

C. The school district's Internet policies and procedures are available for review by all parents, guardians, staff, and members of the community.

D. Because of the rapid changes in the development of the Internet, the school board shall conduct an annual review of this policy.

Legal References:
17 U.S.C. 101 *et. seq.* (Copyrights)
15 U.S.C. 6501 *et. seq.*
Children's Internet Protection Act of 2000 (CIPA) 47 U.S.C. 254
47 C.F.R. 54.520 (FCC Rules Implementing CIPA)
Title III of the Elementary and Secondary Education Act of 1965, 20 U.S.C. 1601, *et. seq.*, as amended.
Minn. Stat. 125B.15 and 125B.25

Cross References:
District 77 Policy 505 (Distribution of Nonschool Sponsored Materials on School Premises by Students and Employees)
Policy 406 (Public and Private Personnel Data)
Policy 506 (Student Discipline)
Policy 515 (Protection and Privacy of Pupil Records)
Policy 519 (Interviews of Students by Outside Agencies)
Policy 521 (Student Disability Nondiscrimination)
Policy 522 (Student Sex Nondiscrimination)
Policy 603 (Curriculum Development District 77 Policy 604 (Instructional Curriculum)
Policy 606 (Textbooks and Instructional Material)
Policy 804 (Bomb Threats)
Policy 904 (Distribution of Materials on School District Property by Nonschool Persons)

Sample

Internet Use Agreement

Student

I have read and do understand the school district policies relating to safety and acceptable use of the school district computer system and the Internet and agree to abide by them. I further understand that any violation of the policies is unethical and may constitute a violation of law. Should I commit any violation, my access privileges may be revoked, school disciplinary action may be taken, and/or appropriate legal action may be taken.

_____

User's Full Name (please print)

_____

User Signature

_____

Date

Parent or Guardian

As the parent or guardian of this student, I have read the school district policies relating to safety and acceptable use of the school district computer system and the Internet. I understand that this access is designed for educational purposes. However, I also recognize it is impossible for the school district to restrict access to all controversial materials and I will not hold the school district or its employees or agents responsible for materials acquired on the Internet. I hereby give permission to issue an account for my child and certify that the information contained on this form is correct.

_____

Parent or Guardian's Name (please print)

_____

Parent or Guardian's Signature

Supervising Teacher

(Must be signed if applicant is a student)

I have read the school district policies relating to safety and acceptable use of the school district computer system and the Internet and agree to promote these policies with the student. Because the student may use the Internet on the school district computer system for individual work or in the context of another class, I cannot be held responsible for the student use of the Internet on network. As the supervising teacher I do agree to instruct the student on acceptable use of the Internet and network and proper network etiquette.

_____

Teacher's Name (please print)

_____

Teacher's Signature

Sample

World Wide Web Page Creation Guidelines

(adapted from Mankato Area Schools, Mankato, Minnesota)

Date:

The availability of Internet access in all *ABC* Public schools provides an educational opportunity for students and staff to contribute to the *ABC* School District's Web pages on the World Wide Web.

The creation of a Web page provides a means of two-way communication for the purposes of sharing information with the *ABC* School District and the world about school curriculum and instruction, school-authorized activities, and other information relating to our schools and our mission; and providing instructional resources for staff and students.

Publishing privileges are provided to students and staff through individuals who have been authorized by the District Media Services. Creators of Web pages need to familiarize themselves with—and practice—the following guidelines and responsibilities, or pages may not be published.

Content Standards

Subject Matter—All subject matter on *ABC* School District Web pages and their links must relate to curricula and instruction, school-authorized activities, or information about the *ABC* School District or its mission. Staff or student work may be published only as it relates to a class project, course, or other school-related activity. Neither students, staff, nor other individuals may use the district's Web pages to provide access to their personal pages on other servers or online services.

Quality—All work must be free of any spelling or grammatical errors. Documents may not contain objectionable material or point directly to objectionable material (i.e., material that does not meet the standards for instructional resources specified in other related district guidelines). The judgment of the teachers, building media specialist, and, ultimately, the District Media Supervisor will prevail.

Student Safeguards—While district policies and related statutes pertaining to "directory information" may allow the release of some personal data about students, we have chosen to establish the following guidelines:

■ Documents shall include only the first name of the student.

- Documents shall not include a student's home phone number or address or the names of other family members or friends.

- Published e-mail addresses shall be restricted to those of staff members.

- Decisions on publishing student pictures (digitized or video) and audio clips are based on the supervising teacher's judgment and signed permission of the student and parent or guardian.

- No student work shall be published without permission of the student and parent or guardian.

- Students shall retain copyright of all originally written materials.

- Copyright on materials written by staff members as a part of their professional duties shall stay with the school district unless other arrangements have been previously made.

Policies

The following additional policies apply to electronic transmission:

- No unlawful copies of copyrighted material may be produced or transmitted via the district's equipment, including its Web server.

- All communications via the district Web pages must have no offensive content. This includes religious, racial, and sexual harassment, violence, and profanity.

- Any deliberate tampering with or misuse of district network services or equipment will be considered vandalism and will be handled as such.

Technical Standards

District person responsible: Director of Media and Technology

In the interest of maintaining a consistent identity, professional appearance, and ease of use and maintenance, the following technical standards are established for all *ABC* School District Web pages. Each Web page added to the district Web site must contain certain common elements:

- At the bottom of the page, there must be the date of the last update of the page and the name or initials of the person(s) responsible for the page or the update.

- At the bottom of the page, there must be a link that returns the user to appropriate points in the district pages. This would normally be a return to the district home page.

- Standard formatting is used; browser-friendly HTML editors or word processor programs that save files as HTML files may be used.

- Care should be used in creating extensive files with tiled backgrounds, large graphics, or unusual or dark color combinations.

- The authorized teacher who is publishing a final Web page will edit, test the document for accurate links, and ensure that the page meets the content standards listed. In addition, the teacher will assume responsibility for updating the links as needed.

- Pages may not contain links to other pages that are not yet completed. If further pages are anticipated but not yet developed, the text that will provide the link should be included but may not be made "hot" until the further page is actually in place.

- All graphics should be in GIF or JPEG format, compressed to minimize size. Other formats, including sound or video, may be used after consultation with the Director of Media and Technology.

Directory structure will be determined by the Director of Media and Technology and the building person(s) responsible for coordinating the school's Web pages. Staff members approved for access will be given access passwords by the Director of Media and Technology.

Revision of Guidelines:

These guidelines will be evaluated and updated as needed in response to the changing nature of technology and its applications in the *ABC* School District.

Code of Ethics of the American Library Association

As members of the American Library Association, we recognize the importance of codifying and making known to the profession and to the general public the ethical principles that guide the work of librarians, other professionals providing information services, library trustees, and library staffs.

Ethical dilemmas occur when values are in conflict. The American Library Association Code of Ethics states the values to which we are committed, and embodies the ethical responsibilities of the profession in this changing information environment.

We significantly influence or control the selection, organization, preservation, and dissemination of information. In a political system grounded in an informed citizenry, we are members of a profession explicitly committed to intellectual freedom and the freedom of access to information. We have a special obligation to ensure the free flow of information and ideas to present and future generations.

The principles of this Code are expressed in broad statements to guide ethical decision making. These statements provide a framework; they cannot and do not dictate conduct to cover particular situations.

I.   We provide the highest level of service to all library users through appropriate and usefully organized resources; equitable service policies; equitable access; and accurate, unbiased, and courteous responses to all requests.

II.   We uphold the principles of intellectual freedom and resist all efforts to censor library resources.

III.   We protect each library user's right to privacy and confidentiality with respect to information sought or received and resources consulted, borrowed, acquired, or transmitted.

IV.   We recognize and respect intellectual property rights.

V.   We treat co-workers and other colleagues with respect, fairness, and good faith, and advocate conditions of employment that safeguard the rights and welfare of all employees of our institutions.

VI.   We do not advance private interests at the expense of library users, colleagues, or our employing institutions.

VII.   We distinguish between our personal convictions and professional duties and do not allow our personal beliefs to interfere with fair representation of the aims of our institutions or the provision of access to their information resources.

VIII. We strive for excellence in the profession by maintaining and enhancing our own knowledge and skills, by encouraging the professional development of co-workers, and by fostering the aspirations of potential members of the profession.

Adopted by the ALA Council
June 28, 1995
© Copyright 1997, 1998, 1999, 2000, 2001, 2002, American Library Association.

Code of Ethics for Minnesota Teachers

MINNESOTA BOARD OF TEACHING
8700.7500
Updated 9/20/01

Subpart 1. Scope.
Each teacher, upon entering the teaching profession, assumes a number of obligations, one which is to adhere to a set of principles which defines professional conduct. These principles are reflected in the following code of ethics, which sets for to the education profession and the public it serves standards of professional conduct and procedures for implementation. This code shall apply to all persons licensed according to rules established by the Minnesota Board of Teaching.

Subpart 2. Standards of professional conduct.
The standards of professional conduct are as follows:

I.   A teacher shall provide professional educational services in a nondiscriminatory manner.

II.   A teacher shall make reasonable effort to protect the student from conditions harmful to health and safety.

III.   In accordance with state and federal laws, a teacher shall disclose confidential information about individuals only when a compelling professional purpose is served or when required by law.

IV.   A teacher shall take reasonable disciplinary action in exercising the authority to provide an atmosphere conducive to learning.

V.   A teacher shall not use professional relationships with students, parents, and colleagues to private advantage.

VI.   A teacher shall delegate authority for teaching responsibilities only to licensed personnel.

VII.   A teacher shall not deliberately suppress or distort subject matter.

VIII. A teacher shall not knowingly falsify or misrepresent records or facts relating to that teacher's own qualifications or to other teachers' qualifications.

IX.   A teacher shall not knowingly make false or malicious statements about students or colleagues.

X.   A teacher shall accept a contract for a teaching position that requires licensing only if properly or provisionally licensed for that position.

CHEATING
and how to avoid it

A student guide to plagiarism, cheating, and intellectual property use in Anytown Public Schools, Anytown USA

- What's Inside?
- Definition of Cheating
- Examples of Cheating
- Why You Shouldn't Cheat
- How We Know You Cheat
- How You Get Caught
- Consequences of Cheating
- How to Avoid Cheating

Based on cheating guideline publication developed by the Battle Creek, Michigan School District. Used with permission.

Sample Plagiarism Guidelines continued

Definition of Cheating:

Anytown Public Schools defines cheating as using some else's words, work, test answers, or ideas and claiming them as your own.

Examples of Cheating:

- Hiring someone to write a paper, buying a paper or project, or downloading a paper from an online service.
- Not properly citing the works, pictures, music, video, or other forms of communication in your research projects.
- Rewording someone else's words (paraphrasing) and not giving that person credit for the ideas you have built on thereby passing someone's ideas off as your own.
- Sharing files (e.g., an Excel worksheet) in a business class.
- Copying math homework.
- Letting your project partner do all the work and just putting your name of the final report.
- Letting your mom or dad build your project.
- Looking at another's test or sharing what is on a test with students in other sections of that class.
- Turning in your brother or sister's old project.

Why You Shouldn't Cheat:

- People's words, work, or ideas are considered "intellectual property"—meaning the creator owns them. Some types of plagiarism not only violate school rules, but state and federal laws.
- You are not practicing skills you will need to know to succeed in college or the workplace: how to write, analyze, form conclusions, or generate new ideas.
- Others will look at you as a "cheater" and your character and reputation will suffer.
- You will feel bad about yourself when you take credit for others' work.
- You will feel good about yourself when you meet the challenges of your school work.

How You Get Caught:

- *New Technology* Teachers and media specialists can simply plug a phrase from your work into a simple search engine and find where in cyberspace you scammed an idea or paper.
- *Teachers Talk* Teachers do talk to one another. You would be surprised to find out that some students have tried to turn in work in one class that their friends have turned in, in another teacher's class.

- *Teachers Remember* Work that was turned in by a friend or relative years before can still be recognized by teachers if you try to turn it in again as your own. When teachers read a set of tests, lab reports, essays, or papers, they do not forget what other students have written. There is a fine line between collaboration and cheating—be aware of it.
- *Teachers Know Your Writing* Teachers know how students write. It doesn't take much to recognize what was written by a particular student or what was written by someone else—say on a Web site.

Consequences of Cheating:

The consequences for getting caught plagiarizing someone else's words, work, or ideas will range from receiving no credit for the assignment until the work is yours to losing credit for the entire class. Check with your teacher and school handbook for more specific information.

How to Avoid Cheating:

- The best way to avoid cheating and plagiarism is to find ways to personalize your assignments. React in your writing about how your topic might personally affect YOU, your family, your school, or your community. An original conclusion which is supported by facts from other works properly cited is never cheating. Write in your own voice, not just in your own words.
- Organize your work so that you don't run into a last minute time crunch that keeps you from studying, writing, creating, revising, reflecting, and making your work your own.
- Keep good records as you do research of where you found your supporting ideas. It's easier than doing research twice—once for finding the information and again for doing the bibliography.
- ALWAYS include a bibliography, list of resources, or acknowledgement whenever you use the work or ideas of others. If you can't provide a citation, don't use the source.
- Understand that using other's work IS permissible and usually necessary to create well-supported arguments, conclusions, and answers to questions. Giving credit to the source of this work keeps it from being plagiarism.
- Make as large a percentage as possible of your work original. Use direct quotes or paraphrasing only when what you find is written in such a way that it clarifies or makes memorable the idea expressed.

Sample Plagiarism Guidelines continued

Choosing When to Give Credit:

Taken from the Purdue University's Web site:
<http://owl.english.purdue.edu/handouts/research/r_plagiar.html>. Used with permission.

Need to document:	No need to document:
When you are using or referring to somebody else's words or ideas from a magazine, book, newspaper, song, TV program, movie, Web page, computer program, letter, advertisement, or any other medium	When you are writing your own experiences, your own observations, your own insights, your own thoughts, your own conclusions about a subject
When you use information gained through interviewing another person	When you are using "common knowledge"—folklore, common sense observations, shared information within your field of study or cultural group
When you copy the exact words or a "unique phrase" from somewhere	When you are compiling generally accepted facts
When you reprint any diagrams, illustrations, charts, and pictures	When you are writing up your own experimental results
When you use ideas that others have given you in conversations or over e-mail	* Material is probably common knowledge if . . . ■ You find the same information undocumented in at least five other sources ■ You think it is information that your readers will already know ■ You think a person could easily find the information with general reference sources

Sample Plagiarism Guidelines continued

Making Sure You are Safe:

Taken from the Purdue University's Web site:
<http://owl.english.purdue.edu/handouts/research/r_plagiar.html>.
Used with permission.

	Action during the writing process	Appearance on the finished product
When researching, note-taking, and interviewing	Mark everything that is someone else's words with a big Q (for quote) or with big quotation marks. Indicate in your notes which ideas are taken from sources (S) and which are your own insights (ME). Record all of the relevant documentation information in your notes.	Proofread and check with your notes (or photocopies of sources) to make sure that anything taken from your notes is acknowledged in some combination of the ways listed below: ■ In-text citation ■ Footnotes ■ Bibliography ■ Quotation marks ■ Indirect quotations
When paraphrasing and summarizing	First, write your paraphrase and summary without looking at the original text, so you rely only on your memory. Next, check your version with the original for content, accuracy, and mistakenly borrowed phrases.	Begin your summary with a statement giving credit to the source: According to Jonathan Kozol, ... Put any unique words or phrases that you cannot change, or do not want to change, in quotation marks: *"savage inequalities" exist throughout our educational system (Kozol).*
When quoting directly	Keep the person's name near the quote in your notes and in your paper. Select those direct quotes that make the most impact in your paper—too many direct quotes may lessen your credibility and interfere with your style.	Mention the person's name either at the beginning of the quote, in the middle, or at the end. Put quotation marks around the text that you are quoting. Indicate added phrases in brackets [ ] and omitted text with ellipses (. . .).
When quoting indirectly	Keep the person's name near the text in your notes, and in your paper. Rewrite the key ideas using different words and sentence structures than the original text.	Mention the person's name either at the beginning of the information, or in the middle, or at that end. Double check to make sure that your words and sentence structures are different than the original text.

If you have any questions whether something you are doing may be cheating or plagiarism, talk to your parents, teacher, or media specialist.

A Good Policy for Policies

Is there any definitive answer to what should or should not be filtered to meet CIPA requirements? Our technology director has been checking more little boxes on our filter. Just yesterday he decided to block Hotmail-type e-mail that students use to contact each other and experts for projects. —Librarian

The administrators in our district have banned the use of cell phones and pagers by all students. I want my daughter to carry her cell phone. With all the school shootings, she needs to be able to call in case of an emergency! —Parent

Teachers and students are saving program files in their online storage areas. Wasn't this set up to be just for documents? Having programs on that server makes it extremely time consuming to search for viruses. I am just going to delete these kinds of files when I find them. —Technician

Most library media specialists and school staff members realize that technology is a double-edged sword. Almost any device can be used in ways that are disruptive, annoying, unethical, and even destructive. Technology is neutral: The same hammer that builds the cathedral can be used to break its windows. Just a few examples:

Technology	Appropriate uses	Not-so-appropriate uses
WWW	Source of great information for school projects	Source of pornography, ready-made term papers, and hate group propaganda
Cell phone	Means of communication in emergencies	Means of disrupting classes
Personal digital assistants	Devices used to carry e-texts, schedules, scientific programs, etc.	Devices used to cheat wirelessly
E-mail	Ability to share ideas with experts, classmates, and teachers	Ability to harass others, waste time, and share ideas with dangerous strangers

For some reason, many schools have not yet figured out how to create good policies and rules about technology use and they end up with complaints like the ones above. Under the worst circumstances poor or non-existent policies have created what seems like a new range war between not cattle ranchers and sheep herders, but between educators (too often librarians) and the technologists. Judging from what I hear, it sounds like the techies are winning by default since they have, as the librarian puts it, the know-how to check "the little box." Knowledge of what is possible and not possible with technological devices combined with a carefully selected sharing of that knowledge gives techies power and credibility and makes rules they would like to set difficult to dispute.

I have a little mantra I often ask teachers, librarians, and administrators to repeat in our district— "Technicians don't make school policy. Technicians don't make school policy. Technicians don't make school policy." It sinks in if people say it two or three times with feeling.

Please don't think I am beating up on technicians. They do indeed have knowledge that is critical to the vital operation of technology in schools. Plus they have the responsibility for data security, network bandwidth conservation, and the reliable operations of what are usually far too many machines for a single person to maintain. My sympathies are with them when they wish to make rules that will decrease the likelihood of more technical problems than are already on a *very* full plate.

Yet these hard-working people often do not understand parent, teacher, librarian, or student goals and concerns. They may not understand why it so important that kids have access to as wide a range of information as possible. They may not understand that teachers need some flexibility to load software for preview on their computers. They may not understand why it is important that the library catalog and online reference sources be available from the homes of students and staff. They may not understand that the librarian needs the password to the desktop security program in the computer lab.

So who in a school *should* ultimately make the technology rules? In our district, these decisions are made by our district technology advisory committee, the same folks that make lots of technology planning and budget decisions. This committee is comprised primarily of educators—teachers, media specialists, and administrators—but also includes parents, students, businesspersons, college faculty members, and public librarians. And of course the committee includes our technical staff for their important input on security, compatibility, and implementation issues. And we *do* listen to everyone. Building technology committees should work in exactly the same way.

This has worked well for us. On the difficult filtering issue, the committee decided that as a result of CIPA, we would install a filter, but it would be set at its least restrictive setting. Any teacher or librarian can have a blocked site unblocked by simply requesting it—no questions asked. Adults are required to continue to monitor student access to the Internet as if no filter were present. The technicians now know that it is the responsibility of the teaching staff to see that students do not access inappropriate materials, not theirs. This is a good policy decision that could not have been reached without a variety of voices heard during its making.

An open dialog about concerns, responsibilities, and priorities related to technology is essential for its successful use in schools. Not everyone will agree with the decisions made, but at least everyone will have a better understanding of why they were made. Educational range wars aren't healthy for anyone— especially the little lambs we serve.

Author Profile

(Photo by Brady Johnson)

Doug Johnson is the Director of Media and Technology for the Mankato (Minnesota) Public Schools and serves as an adjunct faculty member of Minnesota State University, Mankato's School of Library Media Education. He writes a monthly column for *Library Media Connection* magazine and has had articles on school librarianship and technology published in over 50 books and journals. He is the author of *The Indispensable Librarian: Surviving and Thriving in School Library Media Centers in the Electronic Age* and *The Indispensable Teacher's Guide to Computer Skills.*

Doug's workshops, speaking and consulting has taken him to Malaysia, Canada, Kenya, Qatar, and Thailand as well as throughout the United States. A list of presentations, his speaking calendar, and many of his writings can be found at <www.doug-johnson.com>.